Peter Handke

Twayne's World Authors Series

David O'Connell, Editor
Georgia State University

TWAS 828

Peter Handke
Photograph copyright Jerry Bauer

Peter Handke

Richard Arthur Firda

Georgia State University

Twayne Publishers ■ New York

Maxwell Macmillan Canada ■ Toronto

Maxwell Macmillan International ■ New York Oxford Singapore Sydney

Peter Handke
Richard Arthur Firda

Twayne Publishers   Maxwell Macmillan Canada, Inc.
Macmillan Publishing Company 1200 Eglinton Avenue East
866 Third Avenue   Suite 200
New York, New York 10022   Don Mills, Ontario M3C 3N1

Macmillan Publishing Company is part of the Maxwell Communications Group of Companies.

Library of Congress Cataloging-in-Publication Data

Firda, Richard Arthur, 1931-
    Peter Handke / Richard Arthur Firda.
    p. cm. – (Twayne's world authors series; TWAS 828)
    Includes bibliographical references and index.
    ISBN 0-8057-8281-8 (alk. paper)
    1. Handke, Peter – Criticism and interpretation. I. Title. II.
Series.
PT2668.A5Z635 1993
838'.91409 – dc20   92-34859
                                                                                  CIP

The paper used in this publication meets the minimum requirements of American National Standard for Information Sciences – Permanence of Paper for Printed Library Materials, ANSI Z39.48-1984.

10 9 8 7 6 5 4 3 2 1

Printed in the United States of America.

Contents

Preface

This book, intended only as a modest introduction and overview of Peter Handke's work from 1966 to 1987, is directed at a general audience without personal access to the German texts, both primary and secondary – the latter of which have assumed the character of a self-generating industry. As Jerome Klinkowitz and James Knowlton point out in their excellent monograph, *Peter Handke and the Postmodern Transformation* (1983), Handke is worth reading and studying for his historic role in initiating the "overthrow" in the 1960s of the European modernist literary tradition.[1] Handke and the Austrian Grazer Gruppe (Graz Group) of writers were pivotal in reviewing both the esthetics and themes of contemporary German-language literature. My book limits itself to a presentation and discussion of the author's work, expanding the coverage and interpretation so ably presented in the primary English-language texts of Nicholas Hern (plays), Jerome Klinkowitz and James Knowlton (prose and novels within the context of postmodernist literature), and June Schlueter (plays and novels). These are all critics to whom I am indebted for ideas and inspiration. In German I have used the following standard commentaries: Manfred Durzak (prose), Manfred Mixner (essays), and Uwe Schultz (plays).

I am grateful to the local Atlanta branch of the Goethe Institute and its representative Handke collection as well as to the Austrian Cultural Institute in New York. The German-reading student of Handke must, of course, begin with the assembled essays edited by Michael Scharang in the Suhrkamp edition and the appended bibliography by Harold Müller. The Schlueter study also contains a useful Handke bibliography for the English-German reader, divided into interviews, general essays, and essays on the plays and novels. With only a few exceptions, readers may spare themselves the time-consuming effort of reading newspaper reviews of Handke's works, the majority of which are repetitive. Handke's plays and books, however, down to his latest theatrical effort, *Das Spiel vom Fragen* (1990), have been the subject of controversial newspaper reviewing, if not controversy. I hope that the present study makes clear where I have borrowed from those numerous writers – and critics – without whom a general book such as this one would have been impossible to sustain.

For all discussion of the primary material I have read both the original German and the English-language translation of the text. To their credit, Handke has been well served by his two English translators, Michael Roloff and Ralph Manheim. Their renderings are highly recommended. A word, however, on the structure and organization of this book. I have followed an arrangement based on those two genres fundamental to Handke's creative and artistic development: plays and prose. Within each generic domain, presentation is guided by a chronological formula. In theater and prose, for example, the reader can expect to find Handke's earliest works discussed first. Chapter 3, discussing Handke's literary theory, is intended as an introduction to the extended chapters on his prose. Though this chapter contains some material anterior to Handke's first plays, it forms a generic piece with Handke's subsequent prose practice, hence its position halfway through the book.

I believe it would be fair to say that Handke's endeavors in the *Hörspiel* (Radio play) and poetry pale when compared with the innovative and historical importance of his position within the context of European postmodernist theater and the novel. Nonetheless, Handke is a creature of the 1960s German-Austrian moviegoing generation and is not only openly identified with filmmaking but has written "cinematic" texts such as *Die Linkshändige Frau* (1976). In any case, the limitations of this study of Handke's writings prevent lengthy excursions into all aspects of his multifaceted career.

In general, my presentation of a particular work aims at the "core" of general critical consensus concerning that work. What critical ideas are considered important in understanding the work? How does the work fit into the program of Handke's contribution as either a playwright or novelist? A reader eager to understand Handke deserves to be led "upwards" from a basal position, ideally reaching his or her own interpretation. Discussion of Handke in German criticism is broad and expansive, representing both traditional and fashionable positions and covering all artistic genres represented in his canon. In English, however, critical interest is centered on Handke's prose writings. For this reason, and for reasons of sheer quantity, much of my presentation has incorporated criticism of Handke drawn from the German and Austrian landscape: books, newspapers, essays, and scholarly articles. Some of the best of these from German and English sources can be found in the Selected Bibliography. Many of Handke's novels and plays are available in English-language translations. These translations exclude some short stories, sundry criticism and the author's first two novels, *Die Hornissen* (1966) and *Der Hausierer* (1967). English-language translations from German critical texts are my own unless indicated otherwise, as are translations of citations from Handke's primary texts (*Die Hornissen* and *Der Hausierer* especially).

Chronology

1942   Peter Handke born 6 December in the Slovene-Austrian village of Altenmarkt (Griffen) in the state of Carinthia. His mother, Maria, is of poor economic origins; both his natural father and stepfather, Bruno Handke, are German enlisted men.

1944-1948   Moves to Berlin with his mother to live with her husband's parents. Goes back and forth between Berlin and Altenmarkt to escape bombing in Germany. To save a deteriorating marriage, all three return to Austria at the end of World War II.

1948-1954   Attends primary schools in Griffen.

1954-1959   Attends the Marianum, a Catholic boys' preparatory training school near Klagenfurt. Unhappy with the educational regimen.

1959-1961   Finishes his studies at a state school in Klagenfurt, where he passes the *Abitur*.

1961-1963   Enrolls for law studies at Graz University in Steiermark (Styria). Active with Forum Stadtpark, a broad-based literary and cultural group. Begins career as a writer and critic. Does free-lance work with Radio Steiermark, the Graz unit of the Austrian national radio network.

1964   "Die Uberschwemmung" is published in *manuskripte*, the house journal of Forum Stadtpark.

1965   Marries Libgart Schwarz, an actress with a Graz theatrical ensemble. Does not take exams for a law degree after completing eight semesters at Graz University.

1966   First novel, *Die Hornissen*, is published by Suhrkamp
            Verlag in Frankfurt. Handke attends Princeton Univer-
            sity meeting of Group 47, denounces current state of
            German fiction, demands changes; is criticized widely
            as self-serving, media-influenced personality. *Pub-
            likumsbeschimpfung* is produced in Frankfurt on 8
            June; *Die Weissagung* and *Selbstbezichtigung* are
            produced in Oberhausen on 22 October. Publishes
            Publikumsbeschimpfung und andere Sprechstücke.

1967   Publishes second novel, *Der Hausierer*, and a key
            essay, "Literatur ist romantisch." *Kaspar* is composed
            and published. Handke is awarded the Gerhart-
            Hauptmann prize by the Freie Volksbühne Berlin for
            Sprechstücke. The short-story collection *Begrüssung
            des Aufsichtsrats* is published.

1968   Moves with Libgart to West Berlin for career reasons.
            In May *Kaspar* is produced in both Frankfurt and
            Oberhausen. Publishes *Hörspiel* in *wdr-Hörspielbuch
            1968*.

1969   Daughter, Amina, is born in West Berlin. Handke helps
            to establish a cooperative publishing venture, Verlag
            der Autoren, to print new works by new authors. Pub-
            lishes *Hörspiel 2* (in *wdr-Hörspielbuch 1969*), *Prosa
            Gedichte Theaterstücke Hörspiel Aufsätze, Deutsche
            Gedichte*, and *Die Innenwelt der Aussenwelt der
            Innenwelt*. Edits a collection of horror stories, *Der
            gewöhnliche Schrecken*. Writes scenario for *3
            amerikanische LP's*, a short film directed by Wim
            Wenders.

1970   Publishes *Wind und Meer*, collection of four radio
            plays. *Quodlibet* is produced in Basel in January. Pub-
            lishes *Die Angst des Tormanns beim Elfmeter*. Moves
            with Libgart and Amina to Paris in February. Writes
            "Chronik der laufenden Ereignisse," a television play.
            Writes and publishes *Der Ritt über den Bodensee*, a
            full-length play.

1971   First German performance of *Der Ritt über den Bodensee* is staged in West Berlin. Mother commits suicide in Altenmarkt. Handke leaves Paris with Libgart and Amina to settle in Kronberg, a suburb of Frankfurt. Makes a lecture tour in the United States.

1972   Handke and Libgart separate; Libgart resumes acting career. Handke publishes *Wunschloses Unglück*, a memoir of his mother's life. Publishes *Der kurze Brief zum langen Abschied, Ich bin ein Bewohner des Elfenbeinturms* (an essay collection), and *Stücke I* (plays). Cowrites film scenario with Wim Wenders for *Angst*, released the same year.

1973   Returns to Paris to live with Amina. Awarded the Schiller prize (Mannheim) and the George Büchner prize by the Deutsche Akademie der Sprache und Dichtung (Darmstadt) for exceptional literary accomplishment. Publishes *Stücke II* and major full-length play, *Die Unvernünftigen sterben aus*.

1974   *Unvernünftigen* is produced in Zürich and West Berlin. Publishes *Als das Wünschen noch geholfen hat*, a collection of poetry and essays. Writes the screenplay for *Falsche Bewegung*, a feature-film adaptation of Goethe's novel *Wilhelm Meisters Lehrjahre*, directed by Wim Wenders.

1975   Publishes *Falsche Bewegung* and the novel *Die Stunde der wahren Empfindung*.

1976   Publishes *Das Ende des Flanierens* (poem), with artwork by Herman Gail. Publishes highly successful novel *Die linkshändige Frau*.

1977   Directs a film version of *Frau* in Paris. *Das Gewicht der Welt*, his first journal, based in Paris, is published.

1979   In October is awarded but declines to accept stipend of Austria-based Klosterneuburg (Franz Kafka prize). Publishes *Langsame Heimkehr*, the first book in the *Heimkehr* tetralogy. Returns to Austria (Salzburg) to live with Amina.

1980   Publishes *Die Lehre der Sainte-Victoire*, the second
              book of the tetralogy. Translates Walker Percy's novel
              The Moviegoer into German.

1981   Publishes the third book of the tetralogy,
              Kindergeschichte, and the fourth, the autobiographi-
              cal text *Über die Dörfer*, a dramatic poem written
              under the influence of Greek classical theater. Co-
              translates Florjan Lipus's Slovene novel *Der Zögling
              Tjaz* into German.

1982   *Über die Dörfer* is produced under Wim Wenders's
              direction at the prestigious Salzburg Festival in August.
              Libgart plays the role of Nova. Publishes another jour-
              nal, *Die Geschichte des Bleistifts*.

1983   Publishes the novel *Der Chinese des Schmerzes* and a
              journal, *Phantasien der Wiederholung*. Awarded a
              prize by the state of Carinthia for cultural and literary
              achievements.

1984   Publishes German translation of René Char's poems
              (1965-75).

1986   Publishes *Die Wiederholung*, an autobiographical
              novel set in his ancestral Slovenia, and a German
              translation of Aeschylus's *Prometheus Bound*. Writes
              Gedicht an die Dauer, a long, philosophical narrative
              poem. *Prometheus* is staged at the Salzburg Festival.

1987   Travels in Japan and Europe. Publishes a fairy tale, *Die
              Abwesenheit*, and a novella, *Nachmittag eines Schrifts-
              tellers*, dedicated to F. Scott Fitzgerald. Co-writes film
              scenario, *Der Himmel über Berlin*. Writes the text for
              the catalog of a Walter Pichler exhibition, "Sculptures,
              Drawings, Model," at the Städtische Galerie, Stä-
              delsches Kunstinstitut, in Frankfurt.

1988   Awarded Austria's highest prize, Der Grosse Oester-
              reichische Staatspreis, for 1987.

1989   Publishes *Das Spiel vom Fragen*, a full-length play.

1990   *Das Spiel vom Fragen* is produced at the Wiener Burgtheater in January. Publishes the essay *Versuch über die Müdigkeit* and *Versuch über die Jukebox*, a short prose piece.

Chapter One

Origins of a Working-class Writer

Peter Handke, born on 6 December 1942 in the village of Altenmarkt (Griffen) in the Austrian state of Carinthia, is no exception to the rule that a person's life is determined by political and cultural factors as much as by personal destiny. In Handke's case, the political and cultural complex was especially important and began years before his birth.

Austrian Carinthia, lying to the south, and Slovenia, formerly part of northern Yugoslavia but now an independent republic, have shared a fretful historical and cultural heritage through centuries of Slavic and Germanic settlement. Occupation and government by outsiders prevailed in alternate periods of German and Austrian-Hungarian rule. A rebellious Slovene majority eventually succumbed to Austrian-Hungarian hegemony, while a Slovene minority in German-speaking Carinthia continued to use its own language and retain its Slavic culture. At the end of World War I the Treaty of St. Germaine awarded a small part of southern Carinthia to adjacent Yugoslavia. By 1920 those parts of Carinthia in a mixed-language area were opened to a plebescite vote. They decided to remain under Austrian rule, and Austrian Carinthia assumed a unique dual cultural identity that continues to this day.

The capital city of Klagenfurt, a trade and tourist center for the surrounding area, has 87,000 inhabitants. Griffen is situated at the foot of a high mountain and contains the ruins of a castle built in 1120. Otherwise, the town of 3,700 offers little else of historical cultural interest. Altenmarkt, Griffen, and Klagenfurt appear as places and backgrounds in Handke's early writings, especially in his first novel, *Die Hornissen* (1966; The Hornets). The Karawanken Mountains lie next to the former Yugoslav border and the Slovene city of Jesenice. Both mountains and city are prominent settings in Handke's novel *Die Wiederholung* (1986; Repetition).

1

Maria Handke, Peter's mother, came from a Slovene-Austrian background. In Franz Hohler's 1972 interview, Handke referred briefly to his 87-year-old grandfather and mentioned his grandmother, who died of cancer in the same room where he had slept as a child.[1] A revealing and depressing portrait of life for Handke's mother is found in his memoir *Wunschloses Unglück* (1972; A Sorrow beyond dreams), where the author's central theme is the effect of the deadening poverty that was the traditional lot of all farmers and peasants in early twentieth-century Carinthia. Handke believes that his mother's suicide in 1971 was no accident but the natural outcome of the social demands placed on poor Slovene-Austrian women by family, community, and class. He finds the religious teachings of the Roman Catholic Church, stressing compliance with state and civil authority, especially culpable.

In *Unglück* Handke says that marital prospects for his mother were improved by the onset of World War II and the subsequent political alliance between Nazi Germany and Austria. Handke's mother, pregnant by her first true love – a German enlisted man and paymaster in the Wehrmacht – was able to marry another enlisted man, Handke's future stepfather, Bruno Handke. *Unglück* contains an account of the first meeting between young Handke and his natural father, a short but sober encounter that seems to have come off well. Peter Handke was the eldest sibling (two younger brothers and a younger sister were to come) (Hohler, 24).

Handke's stepfather had not objected to the peculiar conditions under which his marriage took place. He was soon sent to the front. Peter Demetz notes that "mother and child went to live with her husband's parents in Berlin but returned to Austria to escape the air raids. After the war [they] went back to Berlin to wait for the return of the husband."[2] Fear and anxiety because of the bombing – but also because of his parents' quarrels – characterized the life of the young boy in Berlin-Pankow, a working-class neighborhood, and created lasting impressions that Handke took back with him when the family of three left in 1948 and returned to Altenmarkt. There is no doubt that the return to Austria was intended to alleviate the family's economic situation and save the marriage. In Altenmarkt Bruno found work as a carpenter in a shop run by his relatives. He would never be singularly independent in any sense of the word. A partial portrait of him appears in *Wiederholung*.

In addition to the influences of his ethnic and family origins, Handke's school and education experiences also made a lasting impression on the future writer. They, too, would shape his social and political ideologies and appear as themes and even esthetic components in much of his work. In Griffen Handke attended primary schools (1948-54) whose programs were standard and uneventful. *Wiederholung* contains an account of a possible autobiographical incident in which the transposition of Handke, Filip Kobal, is forced to confront a bully, his first enemy, an event that stamps itself in the narrator's mind forever. From 1954 to 1959 Handke lived and studied at the Marianum, an upper-level institution (*Internat*) organized as a Roman Catholic preparatory school for future priests. This school, lying in the area of Tanzenberg near Klagenfurt, was structured academically as a humanities-based state school (*Gymnasium*) with traditional subjects: geography, history, and classical languages. Admittance to this institution was gained through examination, and one can assume that acceptance was an honor for a poor boy from a rural Austrian village. Graduation would ensure position and status in the community. Slovene-Austrians were practicing Roman Catholics and priests were respected moral and ethical preceptors in their congregations. This interlude with the unbending Catholic fathers, however, was traumatic and destined to end in disaster for a number of reasons.

"Ein autobiographischer Essay" (1957; An Autobiographical essay) stands as a bill of indictment against the conservative, self-serving educational curriculum of the *Internat*. Written in 1967, about eight years after he had left the school, Handke took specific aim at the "lies" and "contradictions" taught in the religious institution's classes.[3] The essay itself has a political agenda and tries hard to subvert the party line and change the system. The *Internat*, Handke argues, supported the goals of the state and its hidden protocol of controlling the poor and social minorities. In Carinthia the objects of this policy were the Slovenes and their despised language, the use of which was interpreted as a challenge to the German-speaking majority. The conclusion of the essay sums up young Handke's inability to absorb and accept the pedagogical indoctrination at the *Internat*: "The apparent outer world, in which I was then living – the *Internat* – was actually an inward one, an outwardly related inner world, and my real self was the only possibility of

relating, in a small way, to the external world" ("Essay," 16). Echoes
of this troubled period in Handke's life also surface in the Austrian
narrator's recollections in *Der kurze Brief zum langen Abschied*
(1972; Short letter, long farewell), in which childhood memory
induces "states of fear" bound to "ways of knowledge." Even in
America, he lives with the remembrance of fear. *Internat* education
leaves its mark, too, on the future writer in *Wiederholung*, Filip
Kobal, who notes his disgust with having spent five years at the
seminary where none of his religious teachers qualified as spiritual
guides. This indictment is doubtless exaggerated, even running
against the more tempered instincts and judgment of Handke, the
mature writer. Priests as authority figures moved about as policemen
and wardens. Reading forbidden authors such as William Faulkner
and Georges Bernanos redeemed Handke's unhappy life at the
Internat, from which his mother rescued him one day under the
guise of maternal duty, an assertion perhaps of parental authority
over her son.

Functioning among the limitations of the *Internat*'s rigid curriculum, Handke moved between the closeted world of the student
seminarian and the routine of assigned compositions, whose themes
he tried to expand by elaborate inventiveness (Hohler, 23). These
early literary sketches were creative daydreams (*Tagträume*) written
under cover, their author like a thief willfully violating rules and regulations. Such endeavors were intended, Handke says, as a counterpoint to boredom, a *"Befreiungsaktion aus einer Fesselung,"* a
gesture of freedom against confinement (Hohler, 24).

Yet, as *Wiederholung* relates, four years at a Klagenfurt *Gymnasium* only intensified Handke's deep feeling of being an outsider, a
deviant student who was instinctively left alone by his classmates,
who, for their part, fell gladly into their future roles as cossetted
young adults of the middle class. In *Wiederholung* one reads that
Handke bonded with his classmates at the *Gymnasium* primarily
through lessons and classroom assignments. This role is assigned to
Filip Kobal, whose character and feelings reflect much of what
Handke has said elsewhere about his own school years. An analogy
is obvious and relevant: Filip, like Handke, is "reduced to silence" by
the social oppression of the educational system. But if study at the
Internat and *Gymnasium* only strengthened the introverted aspiring
writer, this was a price that he understood and accepted, for social

conformity had never been a part of his plan to be a creative writer. As Handke in fact told Hans Ludwig Arnold in 1976, "My goal was always to live as a writer."[4]

His calling as a writer thus preceded any other career choice, especially that of lawyer. A career as a priest was out of the question, and he would never escape the outer trappings of a writer's vocation, the high seriousness, perhaps, of a writer overly dedicated to art, as his early critics accused him of being. From the *Internat*, however, there were long-lasting positive influences, to wit, that institution's stress on self-discipline as a writer's prerequisite for personal and artistic survival. The suppressive nature of the *Internat* regimen taught him the complexity and the structure of the "inner world" as opposed to the "outer world." Leftist critics, such as Michael Springer, have attacked Handke's early writerly obsession with portraying the overly formalistic, the subjective self-analysis of his heroes and heroines. Those faults are attributed easily to the *Internat* experience, says Springer, and were assimilated by Handke at a cost to his viable connection to an outer world.[5]

Handke's decision to study law was due to external considerations. Both Arnold's and Hohler's interviews point out that, as a recent graduate of a *Gymnasium*, young Handke realized he was at a vocational crossroads. He was academically prepared to begin his legal education, but he did not know how to reconcile his instinctive love of writing with the economic imperative of choosing a life-style or career through which a writing vocation might be feasible. As Arnold notes, Handke was saved by a helpful German teacher who explained that studying law could give him the free time to write.

From 1961 to 1965 Handke studied at the Karl-Franzens Universität in Graz.[6] Graz – a Slavic word that roughly translates as "small fortress" – was then and still remains the capital city of Steiermark (Styria) a state in southeastern Austria. Graz's ancient history, dating back to 1240, and its historical quarter, the site of Graz University, make the town of 243,000 inhabitants dear and memorable to tradition-loving Austrians. Manfred Mixner, quoting Alfred Kolleritsch, has written that Graz was always a deceptively romantic city, a place content to hide its tendencies toward cultural novelty and change under the veneer of sentimental Austrian culture.[7] In the early 1960s, when Handke matriculated, both the town and the university were catalysts for a force calculated to stimulate modernity and renewal in Austrian art: the Forum Stadtpark. A *Künstlervere-inigung* (artists' club) of many persuasions, it served as a home for new art and sponsored inventive, nontraditional artists and writers, like Peter Handke.

At Graz, Handke completed eight semesters of required study but did not complete the third mandated, state-administered law examination (*Staatsexamen*). He was writing and working as a hired critic for Alfred Holzinger, a literary editor for Radio Steiermark. In the summer of 1965, shortly before the date of the third law test, Handke's first novel, *Die Hornissen*, was accepted by the prestigious West German publisher, Suhrkamp Verlag. This event effectively and practically cancelled any serious consideration Handke may have given to starting a career as a lawyer. It seemed that he attained overnight the unusual honor of being placed in the publisher's list-ing of modern German classic writers, like Hermann Hesse, Robert Musil, and Robert Walser, to name only a few. Handke may have enjoyed the intercession of friends and associates from the staff of *manuskripte*, which publication was the leading Austrian vehicle for experimental prose and poetry.

With the publication of *Die Hornissen* in 1966, Handke's career as a writer truly began; this career over the last 25 years has been marked by economic and artistic independence. Especially contro-versial in some quarters of the postwar German literary establish-ment was Handke's unique appearance in April 1966 at the twenty-eighth meeting at Princeton University of Gruppe 47 (Group 47), the group of leading German-language writers, who had first come together in 1947 to read and critique each other's work. They had been drawn toward the moral and ethical renewal of German lan-guage and literature. The group consisted of major novelists, drama-tists, and poets – including Siegfried Lenz, Ingeborg Bachman, Günter Grass, Peter Weiss, and Uwe Johnson – who were intense defenders of German literature as a vehicle of social regeneration. Ironically, Group 47 had been meeting yearly for about 28 years and had become an institution itself, with a formula for literary esthetics: in general, to avoid the extravagance of form and support descrip-tive, realistic content. Handke, who was an impetuous 24-year-old at the time of the Princeton meeting not only had the temerity to chal-lenge the strategic direction of Group 47's literary platform; he also read excerpts from *Der Hausierer* (1967; The Peddler), his second novel, a difficult, reader-unfriendly text purporting to deconstruct the genre of the crime novel. From the beginning of his literary career Handke had a flair for publicity, for sensing the future direction of not only the marketplace but also the avant-garde. He was on the cutting edge of literary experimentation, positioning himself as a founder of the Austrian postmodernist esthetic temperament.

Handke and his new wife, the Austrian stage actress Libgart Schwarz, left Graz for Düsseldorf in the spring of 1966. Handke was on his way to tend to the premiere of *Publikumsbeschimpfung* (1966; Offending the audience) at the Frankfurt Theater am Turm in June during its first "Experimenta" theater festival, a week-long series of European experimental plays and a prestigious program of new dramatic works on the cutting edge of creative theater. That Handke's *Publikumsbeschimpfung* was both successful and controversial is now part of contemporary German theater history. The "offense" of the audience lay primarily in Handke's refusal to validate the "reality" of 1960s theater: illusion, subjectivity, and political indoctrination. Handke was again the center of critical and vindictive notoriety, as he had been in Princeton when he attacked the literary establishment.

After this singular event, Handke and Libgart bought a "permanent" home in Düsseldorf that they hardly used. In 1967 they moved to West Berlin, where they lived for two years and where their daughter, Amina, was born in 1969. They made the move to Berlin for the sake of both careers. In Berlin Handke tried, ineffectively, to join a group of young socialists, but this gesture of ideological solidarity failed; moreover, Libgart's continuing evening appearances at the Volksbühne theater made Handke's role as a babysitter a necessity. He did, however, join creative and communal forces with ten other writers in 1969 to found the Verlag der Autoren, an independent publishing house. The Verlag not only supported radical writers but took figures like filmmaker Rainer Werner Fassbinder under its wing. Handke would publish his television play, "Chronik der laufenden Ereignisse" (1970; Chronicle of current events) and several radio plays with this group.

Revelatory details of the ongoing personal and artistic changes in Handke's life at this time can be found in the pages of *Kindergeschichte* (1981; Child story). Especially upsetting for Handke, as the book intimates, was his realization that with the birth of his child he would have to make a radical adjustment in both his personal and professional lives. Though Handke refers only indirectly to himself and others in *Kindergeschichte*, the autobiographical slant of this text is unmistakable: Handke appears in the book as "he." We read that "he" was not prepared emotionally for his new role as a father, that he felt trapped in domesticity. In short, he felt he deserved sympathy. This novel also suggests that Handke was beginning to doubt that he and his wife were right for each other and to wonder whether his marriage was a mistake. Hostility between himself and his unencumbered unmarried friends also increased. He was convinced that these friends were hostile toward children and related parental obligations. *Kindergeschichte* proposes that the Berlin period of Handke's life was a loveless time, and that his subsequent decision to go to France was a move calculated to improve his marriage through a change in setting. Handke, his wife, and their child thus went to Paris, but they would, of course, experience a city different from the place of fantasy the young childless couple had known before on short visits.

An informal picture published in the German weekly *Der Spiegel* in 1970 shows Handke in Paris as the happy paterfamilias, living in the Montmartre quarter of the city. The accompanying article summarizes his phenomenal success.[8] This was a productive and creative period for Handke. He finished several experimental radio plays and one television script, "Chronik der laufenden Ereignisse," a freely constructed record of images, news events, and happenings. In Paris he also wrote the text for a long play, the experimental *Der Ritt über den Bodensee* (1970; The Ride across Lake Constance). Finally, Suhrkamp issued his phenomenally successful novel *Die Angst des Tormanns beim Elfmeter* (1970; The Goalie's anxiety at the penalty kick), which was published in English in the United States in 1972. The work shows not only Handke's skill in genre manipulation but his talent for adapting issues of linguistic and semiological concern to fiction.

Kindergeschichte provides further biographical background to Handke and Libgart's decision to leave the hustle of Paris and move in 1971 to Kronberg, a wooded Frankfurt suburb. They wanted to rear their child in a different environment, and to this end they chose to live in a modern, custom-designed house. The project was organized by Libgart, and Handke did not see his new home until it was nearly finished, a portent perhaps of further marital disinterest or a sign of a secret wish for solitary living. As *Kindergeschichte* indicates, a separation but not a formal break soon took place. Libgart returned to her stage career but visited the child in those first several months of separation. For all intents and purposes, Handke was left with the permanent care and custody of his young daughter. His feelings over Libgart's departure are veiled in privacy, but he was generous and respectful toward his wife's professional ability. In 1982 she appeared in a leading role in a production of Handke's dramatic poem *Über die Dörfer* (1981; Through the villages) at the Salzburg Festival, a singular honor for any European actress.

Charles Linder's interview with Handke at Kronberg in 1972 portrays the "bachelor" author and suggests Handke's unhappiness with his sterile environment, his mistaken assumption that he could live and work "in a place that is strange and in which I feel a stranger."[9] He was ready to return to Paris! The Kronberg house, an emotional burden, is the locus of Handke's long prose poem, "Leben ohne Poesie" (1972; Life without poetry), a work that illustrates in rambling language the existentialist crisis and subsequent rebirth of a man confined to a life of predictability, without the creative stimulus of art or city life. The routine of his life at Kronberg, however, was broken by routine readings of his work in cities like Vienna, Amina in tow. An interview with Karin Kathrein in *Die Presse* reveals his interest in Viennese city life and his unhappiness with Kronberg.[10] The banality of Kronberg also characterizes the setting of Handke's best-selling novella *Die Linkshändige Frau* (1976; The Left-handed woman), which recounts the loneliness and austere life of a woman rearing her child alone after she decides to separate from her husband. This is on the surface an objective and sympathetic literary text with no political agenda. That it should have some direct or indirect relevance to Handke's personal life, however, is perhaps no accident. It is a work in which place and context are factors in its narrative resolution.

In 1973 Handke returned to Paris, where Amina continued her education in French schools. This second long stay would last until 1979. In Paris Handke published a Paris-based novel, *Die Stunde der wahren Empfindung* (1975; A Moment of true feeling), directed a film version of *Frau*, and maintained a journal later published as *Das Gewicht der Welt* (1977; The Weight of the world). *Gewicht* is an

excellent, meticulous rendering of Handke's personal "acts of perceiving" in the city, not a predictable listing of a visitor's reactions to
places and buildings. This journal, however, is valuable not only as
an insight into the intimate details of Handke's persona; it is a pre-
liminary step in the exploration of those creative and cultural
reasons leading to Handke's return, with Amina, to Austria and
Salzburg in 1979. In an issue on modern Austrian writing discussed
by Hans Haider in *Die Presse* (1978), Handke states his vision of Austria as a thesis and subject for art and shows his estrangement from
the corruptions and triviality of Austrian life. He feels the need to
find "another country," another Austria beyond sociology and television.[11] This Austria, he asserted in an interview initially conducted by
the young Parisian literary scholar Nicole Casanova (and from which
Haider quotes), will be found in language – that is, revealed in the
process of writing itself. He referred explicity to the literary model of
the English writer John Cowper Powys in *A Glastonbury Romance*
(1932).[12] Handke's interview reveals that his Paris sojourn was, in
fact, the catalyst for those ideas informing the texts of the *Langsame
Heimkehr* (Slow homecoming) tetralogy, Handke's restructuring of
personal and historical destiny in the style of a mythmaker and fabu-
list. The cosmopolitan settings of Frankfurt, Düsseldorf, Berlin, and
Paris were abandoned to focus on the relationship of the narrator
(Handke) to a sense of place determined by regional tradition and
ethnic definition, the retrieval of cultural memory and personal
identity.

In the tetralogy Handke emphasizes the cultural and historical
apprehension of the continuity of experience, and he takes on the
traditional writer's role as a moral and ethical commentator. He had
read and absorbed the lessons of great classical literature taught by
figures like Hölderlin and Goethe, both of whom were original
creators and interpreters of language and tradition. Yet as Norbert
Gabriel rightly says, a distinctive Austrian element has never been
absent from Handke's early writings, especially his novels, where it
was subjected to postmodernist dissection and criticism.[13] Gabriel
insists that life abroad for Handke in Frankfurt, Düsseldorf, Berlin,
and Paris was an opportunity to reconcile himself to his Austria
birthplace. He would learn to suffer his position as Austria's most
renowned living writer, a title that he fears marginalizes him. As he
said in response to June Schlueter's probing question in this regard:

"I consider myself a German-language writer and I am Austrian. That is the answer. And somebody else can by all means call me an Austrian writer. That is also true. But I can only say I am a German-language writer and I am Austrian."[14] This reply reminds us of the contention of both François Mauriac and Graham Greene that they were not "Catholic writers" but "Catholics who write novels."

In recent years Handke's exemplary career as a prolific prose writer has interested many readers and critics. Though he is clearly a writer who prefers to let his creative output speak for himself, three recent prose texts continue to reveal aspects of the man beyond the mask of the artist, the figure beyond the cover of celebrity. *Der Chinese des Schmerzes* (1983; Across), *Wiederholung*, and *Nachmittag eines Schriftstellers* (1987; The Afternoon of a writer) contain self-referential ethnic and cultural elements pertinent to Handke's struggle to achieve personal and creative independence. *Wiederholung*, a thinly disguised family portrait, is concomitantly the story of the origins of a storyteller – namely, Handke himself. In *Nachmittag* Handke appears as the matured and seasoned writer who suffers a moment of anxiety over the viability of his profession in the real world of nonreaders. *Chinese*, on the other hand, contains a solitary, meditative figure with more than a streak of misanthropy, a crosser of thresholds, an amateur archaeologist. The setting of *Chinese* is none other than the environs of Handke's home in the Mönchsberg Mountains, outside Salzburg. The thresholds symbolize political and personal crises and their resolution. In this novel Handke appears in the figure of the "suffering Chinese," a metaphor for insight and resentment born of inner wisdom.

A diverting but unsuccessful aspect of Handke's career in Salzburg has been a trio of classically inspired theatrical productions at the Salzburg summer festivals from 1982 to 1990. These plays include the dramatic poem *Über die Dörfer*, a translation of *Prometheus Bound* (1986), and *Das Spiel vom Fragen* (1989; The Play of questions). Many Handke enthusiasts have not endorsed his efforts to create a working concept of classicism for contemporary theater. The author's 1982 journal, *Die Geschichte des Bleistifts* (The Story of a pencil), records the reasons he was drawn to the literary and philosophical models of classical antiquity. His ability to consult the original texts supports his interpretation of Greek and Roman literature. *Dörfer* is a curious attempt, however, to construct a work concerned with contemporary issues (family, environmental) in language derived from the antique classical style, while *Prometheus* ostensibly examines methodology, how Aeschylus "tells" the narrative of his drama. *Spiel*, on the other hand, shows us Handke again as a rhetorician as he plays the entire range of "questions" in the registry of human experience; it is a philosophical excursion that taxes the viewer's patience.

In addition to these philosophical, introspective novels and plays, Handke has also tried his hand as a translator and middleman for Slovene-Austrian literature published in Carinthia. His translation into German of Florjan Lipus's novel *Der Zögling Tjaz* (Young Tjaz) was published in Austria in 1981. Lipus, a close friend of Handke's, is also a former *Internat* student. For his work as a translator of Slovene literature Handke was awarded the Kärtner Kulturpreis (Carinthian Culture Prize) in 1983. Many other prizes have been awarded to Handke over the recent years, recognizing him as Austria's best-known contemporary writer. Various political constituencies of Austrian city, state, and federal governments have joined in this recognition. Shortly after his return to Austria in 1979 from France, Handke was honored as the first recipient of the Franz Kafka Prize (Klosterneuburg). He passed on its financial stipend to two other writers then living under economic exigency. In 1986 he was given a prestigious award from the city of Salzburg, and in 1988 the federal government gave Handke the Grosse Österreichische Staatspreis (Great Austrian State Prize) for overall excellence in artistic achievement. If the Austrian establishment has thus honored Handke with one of its highest signs of recognition, that society has clearly met Handke on his own terms: singularity and originality that have carried his name far beyond the boundaries of his native Carinthia.

Chapter Two

Theatrical Experiments

Early Theater, 1966-1967

Though Peter Handke had published an experimental novel, *Die Hornissen*, in 1966, it was the premiere of his first play, *Publikumsbeschimpfung*, in that same year that established his name as an innovator in modern German theater.[1] *Publikumsbeschimpfung*, first performed on 8 June 1966 at the leftist-oriented Theater am Turm in Frankfurt under the direction of Claus Peymann, is the first work in a collection of *Sprechstücke* (Language plays). The German word *Sprechstücke* recalls the focus in a language play on words, sentences, and language as primary reasons for writing and viewing a play.[2] The underlying experience for the viewer-reader becomes clear only as he or she confronts the play on the stage or reads it as a printed text. Jerome Klinkowitz and Jerome Knowlton note that "linguistic deconstruction" in this play (as in other *Sprechstücke*) creates a sense of radical familiarity, and that in Handke's subsequent language plays, "a fully formed yet nonillusionistic world is being made on stage" (107). There is little here to which the audience can relate from concrete experience. Other *Sprechstücke* written by Handke from 1964 to 1967 are *Die Weissagung* (1966; Prophecy), *Selbstbezichtigung* (1966; Self-accusation), and *Hilferufe* (1967; Calling for help).[3]

In *Publikumsbeschimpfung*, as in the other language plays, Handke is preoccupied with nothing less than a total renewal of German and European contemporary theatrical conventions. His language plays depart from traditional theatrical components of theme, plot, character, and structure. They do not relate to those models of antitheater found in Samuel Beckett's *Waiting for Godot* (1955) or even the parody of surrealism in Eugène Ionesco's *The Bald Soprano*. Nor do Handke's language pieces use Bertolt Brecht's

13

concept of *Verfremdung* (alienation) as a basis for the audience's assessment of reality and political change. Never entirely political in a programmatic way, as Brecht is in *St. Joan of the Stockyards* (1929-30) or even *Mother Courage* (1941), Handke regards his language pieces as "prologues" to drama.[4] In *Publikumsbeschimpfung*, for example, his actors make a point of telling the spectators that the play is only a prologue (*Vorrede*) to what they did in the past and are doing in the present. The audience itself is the topic of the play (*Publikumsbeschimpfung*, 42).

The language plays are short works and reveal Handke's debt to the Austrian post–World War II language and literary renewal associated with Vienna and Graz.[5] He was a follower in his early work of Ludwig Wittgenstein, the linguist-philosopher, and as one of the earliest figures of the Austrian literary scene centered at Graz University in the 1960s, Handke subscribed to the idea that the writer should "manipulate" linguistic structures and in that process reveal the social mores and behavior that govern language consciousness. The *Sprechstücke* question whether theater, any theater, can replicate the reality of the outside world. Handke's answer in the language plays, as well as in his later plays is a resounding "no," since he believes that in drama language is basically an artificial linguistic construct. Further, language and truth in theater must be constructed anew for each play and each performance, so a playwright's claim to reality is a false one. The average theatergoer, Handke asserts, fails to grasp the "lies" of the theater. Hence Handke's startling position that if the theater teaches us anything, its lessons relate to the mendacity of language and the underlying social institutions that govern it. Incorporated into these institutions is society's untrue assumption that drama and theater can be guides to a higher morality. It is interesting that Handke would reject such idealistic tragic dramatists as Goethe, Friedrich von Schiller, Jean Racine, and Pierre Corneille. For Handke, theater only creates language awareness of the present, with the subsequent social awareness. The viewer has no choice but to question traditional modes of language and social thinking as reflected in the art of the past (Hays, 351).

Publikumsbeschimpfung

The German director Claus Peymann relates that in the spring of 1966 he was asked to read the script of a work that turned out to be

Handke's *Publikumsbeschimpfung.*[6] Peymann admits that both he
and his actors at the Frankfurt Theater am Turm were at first skeptical that the play was the right vehicle for his company. They ques-
tioned Handke's commitment to leftist revisionist art. The manager of
the Suhrkamp Theater Book Company, Karl-Heinz Braun, had been
enthusiastic, however, in his support for Handke's play, despite its
previous rejection by other German regional and national theaters.
The producers and artistic directors of those theaters were not
amused by the prospect of mounting a play that promised to offend
its audience. Only when the supporters of Experimenta I, the
experimental theater project in Frankfurt, came through with a guar-
antee of funding did Handke's first play get both a hearing and a
staging. Peymann concludes sardonically that his company's production turned out to be the theatrical event of the year.

The opening night's German audience was first treated to a
clever argument against conventional theater. Four performers attack
the audience about the nature of theatergoing. Theater tradition and
theater as a private fantasy symbolizing existence are two of the several themes found in the lines directed against the viewers. The
actors do not exempt themselves from this criticism.

This "assault" is accomplished by literally reversing the traditional roles of actors and audience. In a one-sided confrontation, the
audience is lectured on its naïveté and credulity – that is, its presup-
positions about the esthetics and reality of drama are challenged at
every step, placed under "review" and "correction." Handke's primary goal is to bring the audience around to his theory that an
involved audience has a fundamental role in the coding and decoding of meaning in the theater. If the meaning of Handke's play is
found in its language and audience consciousness, then his words at
the end of the play are an important component of the lesson for the
audience about the meaning or nonmeaning of words themselves. At
this point the four figures announce that the audience will be
offended and that offensive language is a means of communication.
Communication of this kind is direct and vital. Barriers are broken
(*Publikumsbeschimpfung*, 44).

The audience is addressed as "thoroughbred actors," "cardiac
conditions," "potential dead," and "sadsacks." The theatrical wall
being torn down is, of course, the wall of trite words that prevents
direct emotional contact and perceptive understanding between

actors and audience in conventional theater. The tirade of offending
words with which Handke concludes his play, however, is not an
arbitrary compilation of insults directed by the playwright against a
particular audience. These words are intended as examples of banal
and stereotypical language. Their use in the play betrays their banality. Their meanings emerge in an acoustical pattern, and this pattern
of sounds, for which Handke has definite instructions, seems to be
of more interest than the invective and insult of the words. If the
language of this tirade can be misunderstood at first by the audience
as street language, it is also unmasked by Handke as the meaningless
language of conventional theater, for it is in a play that we first hear
them. The listener is tempted to use his or her own experience in
decoding their apparent references to recent political German history and allusions to Nazi rhetoric, leftist diatribes, and right-wing
propaganda. In a 1970 interview Handke warned that the words in
Publikumsbeschimpfung are in the nature of artifice and dra-
maturgy, that his point was to use words to "encircle the audience,
so that they would want to free themselves. . . . What is said does not
really matter. I reduced the play to words because my words are not
descriptions, only quotations."[7]

The insults are least effective in giving the appearance of reality,
one engendered from the facts of history, religion, and politics. That
the words stand out so strongly for the viewer, however, is the result
of Handke's deliberately austere dramatic technique of reducing his
play to the essentials. *Publikumsbeschimpfung* has no plot, characterization, or scenes. There are only words whose sounds do not
refer to anything seen on the stage. The audience is forced to rely
upon those words and their underlying falseness in the tirade.
Handke is here close to Brecht in the goal of renewing audience
consciousness, yet there is an essential difference between the two
dramatists – namely, that while Brecht's theater calls finally for
political change, Handke's makes the audience aware that theater is
a catalyst for insight into language awareness brought about by
deliberate artifice created by the dramatist himself.

Die Weissagung

Die Weissagung (Prophecy), another language piece, was actually
written in 1964, a year earlier than *Publikumsbeschimpfung*.[8] Four
months after the 1966 premiere of his first play, however, *Weissa-*

gung and *Selbstbezichtigung* were given a joint performance by the Städtische Bühne in Oberhausen, Germany, presumably because his first play had demonstrated the popularity of their author. His suc-cess came about despite the reservations of many German theatrical critics about Handke's future in the theater. They resented the sensa-tionalism surrounding his name and recalled the arrogance with which he spoke out against Group 47 at that group's meeting on the Princeton campus in 1966. Handke was accused of staging his press conferences and of having written an unreadable novel (*Der Hausierer*). Handke, these critics proclaimed, would never be accepted by the fussy, well-educated German theatergoing public. Time itself has shown that early critics of Handke seriously under-estimated both his originality and his talent.

In a short note to *Weissagung*, Handke says that of all his lan-guage pieces this one is the most formalistic, that the viewer is directed toward language in a way that shows "every sentence is meaningless in the sense that this sentence is independent of any other. *Weissagung* has no meaning, neither a deep one nor any other. . . . I strove only for a density of sound"(*Weissagung*, 204). Despite Handke's denial of any meaning in *Weissagung*, a viewer will persist in searching for meaning in the work, if only from curiosity about the nature of Handke's theater.

Weissagung consists of sentences that, in their totality, are actu-ally listings or predictions about the future read by several speakers. These prophecies, the listener soon finds out, are predictions bound to be true: nothingness will become nothing, as rain will turn into rain. Handke's tone in the play is apocalyptic, owing to the abun-dance of biblical imagery: the inevitability of disease, the fires of Hell, people dying, bombs crashing, and the Last Judgment. *Weissagung*, however, offers another source of interest. As a language piece it emerges as a "presentation of metaphors" that purport to describe reality, yet these metaphors mean nothing, as Handke has noted, since the reality to which they refer lacks any definite reference to the truth. Examples of this technique, so common in the text, are the references to the conduct of "average citizens" and the sound of cut trees. Shoes fit the feet for which they were made. The solemn recital of the lines themselves, recited by the speakers out of context, is intended to contrast with audience expectations.

It has been suggested by Schlueter that the listings of prophecies are metaphors of obvious and trite comparisons, whose originality and meaning have long vanished through overuse and familiarity (1981, 28-29). The author has complained about the necessity of making odious comparisons or parallels, for example, between moviegoing and theatergoing, a language choice that he regards as impossible or meaningless, as it is for using banal metaphors in literature.[9] Schlueter has noted that the "prophecy" of Handke's play is actually his fear that the world of reality, found in the underlying meanings of words, will drown in language nausea, the consequence of surrendering oneself to meaningless words and sentences while doing the world's business (1981, 30). This might occur in a future world of words, pointless metaphors and observations portraying a primary intention of Handke's play. *Weissagung*, as another language play, is related to his goal of examining the bases of linguistic structure found in his other early plays, but it restricts itself to a unique examination of the ways in which people alienate themselves from language through hollow metaphors and word comparisons.

Selbstbezichtigung

While Handke's first play focuses on the renewal of theater and audience expectations in that theater, and *Weissagung* on the abuse of language through trivial metaphors, *Selbstbezichtigung* is concerned with the castigation of the self through interiorized domination (Nägele, 331). In this work, often considered a prelude to *Kaspar* (1967), Handke's first full-length play, two speakers alternately recite a list of crimes, sins, and transgressions committed by an "I" against society. This "I" is not a specific individual but a generalized, grammatical identification related to man as a whole. The transgressions "committed" and "confessed" fit the general code of social expectations. A development in time is followed and, as Hern has noted, "the piece falls into three sections of two to three pages each, followed by a final section of some thirteen pages. The first section, consisting of the first thirteen paragraphs, begins with the statement: 'I came into the world.' . . . 'I' as 'I' tells how 'I' was born and then proceeds to recount . . . the various stages of growth to full possession, awareness and enjoyment of the most important of the faculties of mind and body" (45).

Selbstbezichtigung emphasizes that forms of speech and, by extension, the social forms they engender are of paramount importance. Each of the work's four sections follows the "I" through a progression from birth to growth, rules, and language indoctrination between the individual and society – the last item showing Handke in a confessional scenario as he goes through the gestures of "asking forgiveness" from the audience for putting them through the regimen of listening to the play itself.

In an early German staging of *Selbstbezichtigung*, a male and a female presented the accusations and self-criticism in the style of medieval religious ritual. At a Frankfurt performance two actors were nude onstage, with only simple masks on their faces. The nudity was not intended to be sensationalistic but to emphasize the open admission of "sins" before the audience, who were confronted with an unadorned stage and an open curtain (Peymann, 50). This play, like Handke's other language pieces, offers no stage barriers between actors and audience.

Hern has written perceptively on the ending of the play: he notes that the work moves from an attitude of penitence to one of proud individuality – "I went to the theater. I heard this piece. I spoke this piece. I wrote this piece" (*Selbstbezichtigung*, 72). This final tone, Hern says, reflects the speaker's realization that "the original sin referred to so often in the piece itself is hardly the Christian doctrine; it is the original sin borne by every individual in his preordained inability to live within the dictates of society" (49).

If this interpretation has merit, as I think it does, then the real achievement of the play lies, as Hern says further, in Handke's having rendered the familiar theme of the individual versus society on a level of abstraction and universality that is new and original (50). In contrast to the traditional devices of characterization and fable that Brecht relies on to make his point about the need for social change, the featureless context of Handke's "I," according to Hern, is an abstract residue of a rebellion carried out, with ironical overtones. The "I" uses words and phrases with the awareness that written and spoken language lead paradoxically to penitence and concomitant confession before the "authority" of social rule and convention.

Nägele has suggested that the work deviates from the pattern of the Catholic confessional. While it is true that Handke's early training at a Catholic school was a pivotal influence on the confessional

aspects of the work, and that in the play offenses against the rules of
society and language are recited to an unseen authority with the
power to punish the transgressor, the petitioner is never named
specifically (Nägele, 331). Handke thus reminds the viewer and the
reader that the play is not intended to be the confession of a single
individual, and that the German title for the play, *Selbstbezichtigung*,
has no definite article before it. The title refers to a general confession of sins, for which anyone might be culpable, especially the
audience itself. More important, perhaps, is that in *Selbstbezichtigung* the viewer is forced to become an observer of himself in the
sense that what he observes during the confession of the "I" is a
mirrored image. The viewer is expected finally to realize that his
identity is defined through the image of the other (society).

Hilferufe

Hilferufe (Calling for help), the last of the language pieces, was premiered in 1967 in Stockholm under the direction of Günther Böch
with a troupe of actors from the Oberhausen Städtische Bühne. The
play lasts about 10 minutes (compared with 35 minutes for the other
Sprechstücke) and is thus dependent on a good stage performance,
for it has even less overt substance than the other language pieces.[10]
Despite its brevity, Handke has written detailed instructions for the
performers and given some insight into its meaning (*Hilferufe*, 91-
92). *Hilferufe* wishes to show the way, by words and sentences and
guesses, to the sought-after word *help*. Speakers in the piece first
play out the game of a need for the word *help* to their listeners
onstage, in a setting devoid of any real need of help. They ask
whether the sought-after word *help* might be found in newspaper
language, in lines from government regulations, or in everyday German. Other inquiries cite language from school lectures, grammar
books, breakfast items, and street noises. The speakers ask their
questions out of context and without their usual meaning, yet with
the hope that the listeners will respond with a "yes" rather than a
loud "no." In the interchange between speakers and listeners,
sound is important: "As always, Handke instructs his actors to use
words as they would use them in a soccer chant, for acoustic effect
rather than for meaning. Aid is not summoned; rather, the speakers
create an ovation to the word 'help' and in so doing teach the audi-

ence a most compelling lesson in language" (Klinkowitz and Knowlton, 117). Handke, however, has pointed out that once the speakers have guessed the word *help*, they no longer need the word itself. As soon as the speakers get the word, that word has lost its meaning. Linguistically the play is directed toward abstracting the word *help* from its usual meaning and showing that this process of abstraction terminates when *help* becomes a "pure" word in and of itself, devoid of any concrete reference. This process of abstraction, Handke shows us, is reflected in the listeners' refusal to guess and in the audience's perception that the game onstage is an artifice, since everything offered is only another guess in an apparent game.

Since both audience and speakers prefer a game of useless words, *Hilferufe* offers, through linguistic deconstruction, a pile of words that either contain no meaning whatever or can be stripped of that meaning. The banal chains of words preceding the correct guess of "help" – "one-way street," "insect repellent," "twenty-five cent towels" – all relate to media and "public" language. As Nägele points out, the word *help* and the German title of the play, *Hilferufe*, relate not only to the word game that is the ostensible activity onstage between speakers and listeners; the plea for help reflects back to the writer Handke in his continual search for words and phrases (332). For Handke, *Hilferufe* is a model search for new literary methods and strategies. Writing plays for the stage and novels for the reading public is a linguistic process akin to that found in *Hilferufe*. "Finding" the right word, for Handke, shows ideally the end of a successful search by the author himself.

Further Technical Experimentation, 1968-1974

Kaspar was Handke's first full-length play.[11] It was premiered in Frankfurt and at the Städtische Bühne in Oberhausen at the same time, 11 May 1968, when the West German government was trying to implement its "emergency law" (Peymann, 51). It was a period of political protest by leftist students in both France and Germany. According to Peymann, actors from the Frankfurt troupe rehearsing *Kaspar* were political activists. As a result of the social turmoil, German audience and critical reaction to *Kaspar* was, to some extent, influenced by exterior events and by the author himself. Like the earlier *Sprechstücke*, however, *Kaspar* eschews overt political commentary and shows technical and thematic continuity with Handke's ongoing examination of linguistic and language process.[12]

Kaspar reconstructs the steps by which an "alien figure," Kaspar, is brought into a world structured by language. Movements and gestures are pertinent technical devices in the play, foreshadowing their subsequent use by Handke in later works. The drama critic Günther Rühle noted the mutual activity of language and movement in the play: "Movement appears before language, but it is language that makes movement comprehensible."[13] The text of *Kaspar* is 65 paragraphs divided into two sets of parallel texts with Handke's commentary on stage directions. Actors' lines are often spoken in tandem with each other. Handke punctuates divisions in the play by changes in lighting or blackouts, the latter being the equivalent of scene changes in conventional dramatic structure. The stage setting and props for *Kaspar* are intentionally "theatrical": their interrelationship does not correspond to their usual arrangement in reality. This is a clue to Handke's audience that *Kaspar* is only a theatrical event and not a "slice" of exterior reality (*Kaspar*, 104-5).

Handke derived the inspiration for the central character from a historical incident: the discovery in 1828 of a child, Kaspar Hauser, in the city of Nuremberg. Hauser's origins, along with his incarceration, had deprived him of human contact and prevented him from learning to speak. His extraordinary background became the focus of several European commentaries, many of them speculative and romantic in temper.[14] For some of these writers, Hauser was a "model" figure and a victim of social injustice; they lamented his fate in a world of burgeoning industrialization. German novelists and poets, such as Jakob Wasserman, Georg Trakl, and Hans Arp, contributed in their writing to the myth of Kaspar Hauser. Feature films on related figures were made by the German director Werner Herzog (*Every Man for Himself and God against All* [1975]) and the French director François Truffaut (*The Wild Child* [1969]).

Handke's play pares away the "story" behind the prehistory and subsequent discovery of a "noble savage." Handke's character, whom he calls only Kaspar, is an abstracted and theatricalized figure brought to "birth" onstage in phases from behind drawn stage curtains (*Kaspar*, 107). Handke notes that Kaspar is not a clownlike fig-

ure but is analogous to a movie monster (*Kaspar*, 104). His instructions thus emphasize the artificiality of Kaspar's character; they ren-
der Kaspar an object of Handke's analysis and show how a "man" is
bound to language and the learning process of that language. In an
interview with Arthur Joseph, Handke has indicated other reasons
for writing the play: "Kaspar fascinated me from the start. . . . For me
this was a model of conduct, building a person into a society's
course of conduct by language, by giving him words to repeat. To
enable him somehow to get along in life, to function, he is recon-
structed by voices, by language models, and instruction regarding
the objects on stage" (Joseph, 60).

As a model of language acquisition, Handke's play is intended to
show what can be done to someone used by society in its role as a
manipulative teacher of language. The starting point for this
"instruction" is Kaspar's one line, "I want to be a person like somebody else once was" (*Kaspar*, 118). This abstract sentence, changed
by Handke intentionally from Kaspar Hauser's original statement that
he wished he could "be a horseman like my father was once," is the
center of Kaspar's language education by the *Einsager* (prompters),
who appear onstage as voices early on, at the first sign that Kaspar's
sentence will fail to mediate between himself and things around him
(Hern, 63). The prompters thus give him the words for chair, table,
and broom (*Kaspar*, 76-77). He is praised by the prompters for his
sentence, yet they disavow the limitations of that sentence itself. As
the prompters begin to speak, they help Kaspar begin making sentences and allude to the safety and comfort of words that relate
"specifically" and directly to objects. It is apparent that the
prompters become not only Kaspar's impersonalized teachers, they
also symbolize their advocacy of the social order achieved by language control.

At a central point in the play Kaspar is rendered silent by the
"dismantling" of his one sentence and the overwhelming profusion
of new words. This silence is intended to indicate the first phase of
Kaspar's indoctrination into language making, a necessary correlative
and a prelude to the second step of starting to speak independently
(Hern, 63). Kaspar is taught by the prompters to use the right sentences and words, the correct language models that help an orderly
individual to make his way in life. In addition to delineating the linguistic and social relationships between language and order, the play

also reveals the underlying affinity between order and space. Tables and chairs that were earlier thrown about on the stage are now rearranged by Kaspar into an acceptable way of perceiving objects. He thus becomes an individual learning to learn order. The prompters next teach Kaspar that words and sentence composition are a viable means of entry into the safe world of "perfect" human beings and the ultimate key to social responsibility. Social responsibility, through an orderly use and perception of language and objects, is also found, according to the prompters, in short, simple sentences with no questions.

The final parts of the play continue the "training" and "reeducation" of Kaspar into the submissive and schizophrenic world of word and object relationships. Here Handke expresses Kaspar's apotheosis as a social conformist with the appearance onstage of similar, masked Kaspar-like figures, a throng of nonsensical, mimetic characters who vacillate between sense and nonsense (*Kaspar*, 103). These figures portend the eventual collapse of Kaspar's previous personality, which, despite its primitive nature, was still of one piece. The new Kaspars ridicule words, make noise, and scorn objects. One of them, in a cunning rendering of Kaspar's original sentence that he would like to be "as someone once was," reverses this line to state that he now desires to join the "crowd." If Kaspar is thus exposed to the gift of language expressibility, he is also exposed to "a greater terror, a realization of the painful inability of language and reality to achieve the perfect union of Kaspar's earlier world" (Schlueter 1980, 29). Kaspar's final predicament, the catalyst that precipitates his fall into "madness," is his realization, achieved through language education, that there is only a tentative and ambiguous connection between a word and its referent. Language learning, Handke says in the play, ultimately reflects the idiocy of language and the language process. Society in general is a willing accomplice in this process, though Handke denies any reference to or criticism of a particular society or culture. To this end, he has said, "In *Kaspar* I criticize no concrete social model, capitalist or socialist. Instead [of] abstracting from modes of speech their basic grammatical elements, I point out the present forms of linguistic alienation. . . . To put it succinctly, in *Kaspar*, history is conceived as a story of sentences" (Joseph, 61).

Indeed, *Kaspar* is an anarchic play only within the framework of what it states about language negation, not of what it implies about politics or political reform. Handke has expressed his nausea at stupid speechification and its resulting brutalization of people. A pertinent artistic realization in *Kaspar* for viewers and readers is Handke's meticulous insight into the relativity and shifting nature of language and phenomena, as separated from a fixed political context. The language "schizophrenia" of *Kaspar* is related to a use of language as "sense," where language is intended as an instrument of power and control, and as "nonsense," where language is the lesser of two evils. *Kaspar* alludes finally to the underlying, hidden, destructive qualities of words and language, especially the corollary that whoever controls thought controls language, too. Vigilance is required when the limits of language are set by the "wrong people," symbolized by the prompters in *Kaspar*. For Handke, the prompters might be any representatives or advocates of a fixed, deterministic social or political system and of the language with which it is identified.[15]

Das Mündel will Vormund sein

The titles of Handke's next two plays, *Das Mündel will Vormund sein* (1969; My foot my tutor) and *Quodlibet* (1970; Whatever you say; feel free) bring forth unexpected allusions to Shakespeare's theater.[16] *Mündel's* title comes from *The Tempest*, where Prospero rebukes Miranda with the words, "What, I say, my foot my tutor!" (I.ii), indicating his astonishment that a subordinate should hint of a change in the status of master and servant. *Quodlibet's* Shakespearean "borrowing" comes from the allusion to *As You Like It* in its title, which is Handke's teasing invitation to take *Quodlibet's* half-heard and partially understood words and sentences as facts. Yet the audience must work as hard in decoding the meaning of both *Mündel* and *Quodlibet* as it does with the *Sprechstücke*, which, in contrast to these two pieces, are entirely language-oriented in their dramatic structure.

Both *Mündel* and *Quodlibet* signal vital shifts in Handke's ever-changing conception of dramatic theory and language practice.[17] These plays stand technically at an intermediate point in the development of Handke's theater and are among those plays in which "gesture" and "movement" are broadly assimilated into the playwright's dramatic technique. In this sense, the gestic language of *Mündel* and *Quodlibet* anticipates the skillful inclusion of speech as gesture in Handke's second long play, *Der Ritt über den Bodensee* (1972). Thematically, *Mündel* is allied to *Kaspar's* message of language as power and control. The play is thus another *Kaspar* in that it is one of Handke's abstract lessons in the politics of submission and dominance. The final outcome in *Kaspar*, one recalls, is a natural consequence of language learning and the articulation of human speech. In *Mündel*, however, Handke has chosen to "articulate" the politics of social dominance in a play without words. The text's theatrical environment is characterized by gestures, sound, and movement. Any meaning that *Mündel* has for the spectator lies not only in his or her skill at "reading" gestures and movement as speech; it lies, too, in a keen sense of visual acuity. As a silent or wordless play, *Mündel* isolates human interchange from any semblance of linguistic or narrative reality. Borrowing a clue from Beckett, Handke's behavioral forms emerge as the main claim on spectator attention: Who is doing "what," and "how" is he doing it? As in Beckett, gesture and movement define character, but most important, Handke's technique in *Mündel* forces the viewer to conclude that the postures of the theatrical stage are identical to those of daily life.[18] The representation of theatrical poses is, among other things, an attempt to present the modes of everyday behavior as poses, too. Carl Weber, who has directed Handke's theater, says that Handke, who has never claimed to replicate reality, nonetheless indicates that theater "has derived its images and conventions from the games played by society, which foots the theater's bill."[19] In Handke's *Mündel* eating food, moving a chair, and tearing paper are simple gestic acts, but they evoke models from the structure of social behavior, even as they might be estranged from general human experience.

Mündel was first performed 31 January 1969 in Frankfurt's Theater am Turm, under the direction of Claus Peymann. It consists of 10 short scenes with very detailed and meticulous directions from the playwright throughout. The opening of the piece, for example, specifies the scenery: the "artistic" (false) facade of a farmhouse with birds flying above fields. In front of the house the audience sees an unidentified object, while next to the reproduction of a farm door a block of wood has a hatchet in it (*Mündel*, 9). There are two characters, a ward (Mündel) and a warden (Vormund), who function as a servant and a master, respectively. Their movements range in the opening scene from the bucolic to the menacing. The warden appears in front of the house and begins to stare at the ward. But the ward only eats his apple, ignoring the warden. Both the staring and the gesture of eating are intentionally drawn out (*Mündel*, 12). The play endeavors to mirror power relationships and through movements and gestures shows the control it is possible to maintain over a person without using words. Seemingly innocent activity, such as the ward's eating an apple, is stopped through the act of "staring down," or "ocular assault," by the warden (Calandra, 35). In *Mündel* trivial activities and gestures abound with the force of spoken and printed words, although a unified meaning linking each scene is elusive. During the second scene, for example, the warden demonstrates his authority over the ward through reading and folding a newspaper at a table. In the fourth scene the warden fills a water kettle with a hose as the ward grinds coffee. At the beginning of a new scene one hears a loud breathing that, at times, is like the breathing of a cornered animal (*Mündel*, 36). Several scenes in the piece can be interpreted as signs of either revolt or submission from the ward: namely, when he throws burrs at the warden's back, or when he stands still as the warden throws bottles, plates, and glasses at him. The conclusion of *Mündel* returns to the farmhouse exterior glimpsed by the audience at the beginning of the play. Now we witness the unveiling of an object, a turnip-chopping machine; the warden provides the ward with instructions in how to use it. Since the previous scenes have been filled with indications of revolt on the one hand and intimidation on the other, what ensues is suspenseful and ambiguous. On the darkening stage we search for a last glimpse of the warden beside the ward. The stage becomes quiet. The viewer does not learn what happens to the warden – he might be dead – after the ward begins to use the machine. In a final moment, the ward, who turns out to be the survivor of this last encounter, is viewed pouring sand into a tub filled with water. He embodies despair and archetypal subservience. June Schlueter offers a convincing interpretation of this final scene when she says that "one thinks of the metaphorical sands of time, recalling the earlier scenes where pages are torn [by the ward] from a calendar, also of Beckett's repeated symbolic use of sand" (1981, 54).

The timelessness symbolized by this final gesture can support the reading of *Mündel* as a political parable, as Hern suggests, or even as a "bleak allegory" of intimidation in the perpetual struggle between one man and another (Hern, 81). German leftist students of the 1960s, furious at having to witness another example of Handke's "dead" theater (a theater of no overt political complaint or ideology), missed the point of Handke's experiment in nonverbal communication. *Mündel* is not only a legitimate exploration of behavioral patterns in the interaction of individuals, it also demonstrates that "the way in which experience is ordered, the way in which daily activities are presented and supervised, defines much of the view we have of ourselves and our relation to the world" (Hays, 358). Handke says that what people do to one another can be found in the multiple and experiential levels of gesture, movement, and sound of which *Mündel* consists. Deprived of dialogue and speech, the spectator is forced to become a primary viewer, confronting images that define surface realities in novel ways to reinterpret the human condition from the entrapment of verbal communication.

Quodlibet

Handke next explored posture as a theatrical device in *Quodlibet*, a short play that premiered in Basel on 24 January 1970, under the direction of Hans Hollmann.[20] In this play Handke demonstrates his continued evolution as an experimental dramatist, challenging his audience to leave the realm of the familiar and the ordinary. For example, *Quodlibet* adapts the principle of auditory hallucination to theater – a borrowing, perhaps, from Handke's earlier play *Selbstbezichtigung*. In *Quodlibet* 10 costumed characters appear on the stage; among them, a general, a bishop, a university administrator, a politician, and several women. They are all from the upper levels of society, and they step forward in their own order and inclination. Viewed by Handke as figures of speech, not actors playing the roles of specific characters, they relate to the grammatical forms of language (*Quodlibet*, 157). Their gestures and movements, in fact, relate to the visual and kinetic element of language that endeavors to make its way through the half-heard and misunderstood words coming from the spoken text. The audience hears sundry questions and answers, conversation, allusions, jokes and stories, and euphemisms. The actors, Handke notes in prefatory instructions to the play, are free to talk about what they have read or experienced, or about what they wish to do in the future (*Quodlibet*, 42). The actors use some words that the audience will understand. These are placed among those words the audience merely thinks it understands. Handke's intent, however, is to have the half-heard or barely understood word intentionally agitate and upset the listening audience. This scheme is a part of the esthetic context of the play.

Michael Roloff's English translation of *Quodlibet* is very successful in rendering "content" from Handke's German text. Roloff states that "more than any of Handke's plays to date, *Quodlibet* requires fairly extensive adaptation to an American linguistic, cultural, and historical environment."[21] "No palms" can be misheard by Americans as "napalm," "hero sandwich" as "Hiroshima," "bicycle path" as "psychopath," "hit" as "two-run hit." Handke has conceived the play as a "single living movement of speech" and, as such, a "theatrical ornament" that is "bound" to elements of everyday linguistic reality (*Quodlibet*, 157). Calandra notes, "In some respects, *Quodlibet* is like an abstraction of all those half-heard and hardly understood scraps of small talk which form the basis of Chekhov's theater, a tapestry of Chekhovian murmur" (57).

After stripping these characters of their history and psychology, Handke indicates that only the patterns of talk remain, set within the gestures and movements so visible on the stage. Though conveying the ambiguity of perceived linguistic reality is the ultimate goal theatrically in *Quodlibet* – and the audience is indeed free to do whatever it likes – the sundry meanings assigned by the spectators to the stream of words and phrases are in fact emotionally determined by pity, tenderness, sympathy, and fury. What the audience "hears," however, relies greatly on its cultural sophistication and perceptive acuity.[22] Some allusions and stories can truly remain meaningless and irrelevant for a viewer in a different realm of auditory and cultural accessibility. An untutored mind, as Schlueter connotes, may in truth "hear" nothing at all (1981, 61). For such a viewer, *Quodlibet* remains only an ambitious technical piece and not a consciousness-raising play working in tandem with the forces of language itself.

Der Ritt über den Bodensee

Handke's 1970 play *Der Ritt über den Bodensee* (The Ride across Lake Constance), a longer work, shows structural and thematic affini-

ties with *Mündel* and *Quodlibet*.[23] Like *Mündel*, *Bodensee* is highly
dependent on the viewer's perception of the underlying connections
between normative and theatrical patterns of everyday behavior. In
Bodensee gestures are as controlled as words, but the relationship in
meaning between the two is one of the least obvious aspects of the
text. As in *Quodlibet*, language in *Bodensee* exists in the context of
semiconsciousness, moving in the direction of language forms rather
than language meaning.[24] The face of "realism" gleaned from the sets
of the opening scenes of *Bodensee* is no less deliberately artistic than
the stylized and formalized shape of the stage settings Handke requires for *Mündel*. In both *Mündel* and *Bodensee* the stage is a place
for theatrical demonstration, an area for showing and teaching. Stage
movement in *Bodensee*, like that in *Mündel*, is purposely intended to
occur in an unidentifiable space with no claim to outer reality. The
theatrical space of *Bodensee* lies within a dream or a nightmare of
the mind – or, as Hern has stated, in the "abyss, this innermost
world beneath a thin veneer of normality, that opens up beneath our
feet when we take *The Ride across Lake Constance*" (94).[25]

Critics of Handke's language plays have noted that these earlier
pieces, despite their singular emphasis on language, nevertheless
contain an underlying core of "social specificity" in that language
structure is related to forms derived from a mediating society: for
example, the idea of language as thought control in *Kaspar*, the insti-
tutionalization of ideologies in *Selbstbezichtigung*, and the rejection
of traditional theatrical esthetics in *Publikumsbeschimpfung*. Yet, as
Claus Peymann has indicated, *Bodensee* "makes the theatre its exclusive theme . . . the play's characters are actors, aging stars" (53).
Peymann, who directed the first German version of *Bodensee* on 23
January 1971 at the Schaubühne am Halleschen Ufer in Berlin,
relates further that, at first, his group of politically conscious actors
were hesitant to take on the play "because it was not politically practical" (53). As Peymann notes, a group of actors finally agreed to
work on the piece. The director conceived that the cast would study
its involvement with the profession of acting, its work as individual
actors and actresses, and its fears and difficulties while acting. Peymann's group thus sensed the absence of a plot in the play and realized that, in a work like *Bodensee* where there is no continuous narrative, only remnants of stories, the viewer and the actor are always
fearful of being thrown off balance, overwhelmed by "the undercur-

rent of nonsense, illusions and dream-fantasy indulged in by the characters" (Peymann, 53). Handke's stage in *Bodensee* is not intended to mirror reality. If this stage is a laboratory, as Carl Weber claims, it is not a laboratory for the proverbial naturalistic "slice of life" but rather a background against which, as in *Mündel* or *Quodlibet*, theater – "pure theater" – and the norms of social behavior meet head-on.[26] This bipartite relationship, shown in the play as an awareness (a consciousness) of reality, is actually, as Peymann notes, "a deadly embrace for the characters in the play through the traps and ties of language. With knowledge of the order and hierarchies of language, communication between the characters becomes impossible" (54).

The five actors in *Bodensee* appear in the simulated "roles" of a lover, a boss, a worker, a buyer, and a seller. These roles are not intended to be understood as realistic portrayals. As in a Brecht play, characterization in *Bodensee* lies more in "acting out" a role (*Verfremdung*) than in in-depth analysis of character.[27] In fact, Handke moves freely to alienate the audience from stereotypical character definition in both the stage and print versions of *Bodensee*; the book version of the play assigns the names of German silent-screen stars to the actors – Emil Jannings, Heinrich George, Elizabeth Bergner, and Erich von Stroheim. Readers of the play must grasp Handke's allusion to the similarities in gestic acting style between early film and what is intended for the book version. In the stage performance of *Bodensee*, however, the silent-film names are replaced by the names of the actors themselves – Mary Smith plays "Mary Smith" – so that whatever is happening on the stage is perceived as clearly happening to real people, who are "acting out" the dialogue. My discussion of *Bodensee* refers of necessity to the book version of the play.

As the curtain opens, the audience is first confronted with the disorienting image of a nineteenth-century room whose furniture is covered with white sheets and seemingly glued to the spot (*Bodensee*, 63). One wonders if the room has been abandoned or was never occupied. Handke's actors emerge from a richly appointed set containing a plush carpet and a wine-red runner that leads down a staircase, glimpsed in the background. This staircase, contributing to the operatic quality of the large room, has both a right and left part. Elsewhere there are tapestry-covered doors. The audience is hard put to identify the style of the room; moreover, it is uncertain whether it is meant to react realistically to an image of wealth or artistically to the selected items of interior decoration. Another element of estrangement is the sight of a woman in blackface finishing her job of vacuuming the rug. She turns off a machine and pulls the white cover from under the chair of Jannings, who begins to open his eyes, as if awakening from a deep sleep. George, described by Handke as "someone behind" a screen, steps out in front of Jannings. Both men are physically fat, heavily made up, and wearing clothes that clearly suggest a costumed film actor of the past.

The "action" of the play begins with Jannings's cracked voice stating, "As I said . . . a bad moment" (*Bodensee*, 65). The antecedent of this comment is probably the end of a dream, yet this is never revealed, only assumed. Jannings points to a cigar box lying on the floor beside him, and George misunderstands the gesture, thinking there is something to see on the box itself. Jannings, playing the role momentarily of someone "caught" in the act of wishing to be served by an inferior, masks his real intention by noting the "reality" of the blue sky on the box. At this point in the play Jannings and George begin to act out their "roles" in *Bodensee*; the analogy is the master-servant relationship in *Mündel*. Dialogue between the two offers examples of language that centers carefully on the relationship between words and gestures, between one's perception and one's interpretation. In this dialogue Handke also interweaves major themes and underlying motifs that show how language conveys power and authority. George refuses to pick up the cigar box and asks Jannings whether he was "dreaming," and Jannings tells him a "dreamt story" about a "misunderstood" gesture, in a restaurant setting, between himself and a friend (*Bodensee*, 66). What "happened" in the story, however, is very much in doubt and seems now to be only a metaphor for winter to Jannings. "Winter kidneys flambé" are mentioned. George questions these "details" and others in Jannings's narrative. There follows a scene characterized by gesture and mime between Jannings and George. Jannings casually turns up the palm of his hand. George looks at the hand, which seems to be "directing" him to the cigar box. George goes to the box and hands it to Jannings (*Bodensee*, 69).

Uwe Schultz, focusing an extended analysis on the above passage, has pointed out the complexity and subtlety of the linguistic and psychological game being played out between George and Jannings (82-83). Dominance and control are two major themes in the foregoing episodes, and in the end Jannings wins, since George does indeed put the cigar box into his hand. The somnambulistic state, however, from which both Jannings and George emerge at the beginning of the play seems to undermine the words of their dialogue. With these overall conditions, there is no certainty that anything said by anybody in the play is truly being said in the real world. The audience is especially estranged from the meaning of the "game" it has perceived. Are the men master and servant, rich and poor, or two competing friends? Dialogue between Jannings and George operates on many levels: the intrusion of dreams into our waking life; the impossibility of speaking about something of which one has had no direct experience (kidneys flambé); the borderline between a story and a real event. The encounter between the men suggests, too, that society gives arbitrary assignments of meanings to "action" for the sake of sanity and communication. For example, when Jannings takes the cigar box from George, there is a brief pause, as if Jannings had expected something else, and his hand "is still extended." Jannings notes that he had "meant" to say something else with his extended hand. He offers a cigar to George, who is surprised at the turn of events (*Bodensee*, 69).

As was indicated earlier, the preceding episodes from *Bodensee* are typical of the remainder of the play: scenes of dominance continue to be played out as a language game between two individuals. Yet the mental and perceptive states of the two men intrude, floating as they do between consciousness and sleep. This reminds the viewer and reader of the title of Handke's play, for the rationality of the men can never be taken for granted.

Though other characters in the play, especially the women, experience similar moments of "death" and "consciousness" as they move between the two worlds of dream and reality (linguistic reality and outer reality), certain episodes of the work focus on their release from these "supposedly free and sovereign systems of communication" (Linstead 1988, 75). Such an incident occurs early on when George, viewing the rings on Jannings's hand, is caught up in a moment of realization, a passionate moment of "true" ownership (*Besitzrausch*) centering on the rings. We are intended to appreciate the distinction Handke is making between George's unmediated role as an "owner" and his role as a "buyer." George makes a short speech looking at the rings, which seem to him "as if they were made for me" (*Bodensee*, 72). He hugs the rings sensually and kisses them. The rings reflect his heart. He perceives himself as the possessor of the rings.

Linstead has noted that these are moments of epiphany (direct, unmediated experience), and that the stage characters in *Bodensee* "go through a series of mimes which deal with hearing a pin drop, seeing the sea actually glisten, seeing someone have totally empty pockets" (1988, 77). Every instance of such direct experience, however short-lived, is intended to free the characters from the weight of linguistic prejudgment and to help them discover that words and sentences need not stand for anything other than themselves. A telling episode of this kind occurs when Porten and Bergner work together to free Bergner from a loss of "self" by using a mirror. Bergner does not know in which direction to comb or cut her hair, and as she attempts to do so, she walks in a direction where no one is and asks for help. It is Porten, however, who "frees" Bergner from this alienated state and moves her into another one in which a gesture and its related phenomenon are free of meaning and definition. The cure is nothing more than talking to each other, recounting direct experience as much as possible within an unmediated language system. Here Handke notes simply that the longer they talk, the more sure of themselves and graceful they become. Their talk is trivial, recalling such simple acts as walking down a stairway or even placing a tablecloth (*Bodensee*, 99).

That episodes of "awakening" consciousness are of brief duration, however, is a central theme of the play. The "conformist" behavior of the Kessler sisters – symbols of moribund, joyless normality – causes the actors to revert to the frozen sea of their original dreamlike state. This retreat, however, is ironic, since the sisters are the epitome of nondescriptive individuals: they are dressed identically, and their uninspired conversation is filled with polite phrases and stock answers. Handke has alerted his viewers that in his play the illusion of being liberated from meanings and interpretations, of placing "a block between sign and interpretation is nothing less than a utopian comedy" (*Bodensee*, 58). In *Bodensee* all the players take a ride across the thin ice separating the rational from the irrational and retreat finally into a passive state. As one of them reaches for something, he stops as soon as he starts. Another tries a gesture that dies instantly. In a few seconds all of them grow rigid, as if freezing to death (*Bodensee*, 154). *Bodensee* probes the fragile structures of linguistic and mental consciousness, exposing the schizophrenia, madness, and dreams that lie just beneath the "order" society has imposed on us all (Weber, 54).

Die Unvernünftigen sterben aus

Die Unvernünftigen sterben aus (They are dying out) was first staged by the left-wing Theater am Neumarkt in Zürich on 17 April 1974.[28] Subsequent performances were mounted in Düsseldorf, Wiesbaden, Freiburg, and Berlin, and the Yale Repertory Theater staged it in October 1979.[29] *Unvernünftigen* is not a play in the experimental language style of Handke's earlier theater; it moves in a more conventional direction. The play has two acts and a cast of eight characters, of whom the central figure is Hermann Quitt, a capitalist entrepreneur. Quitt, whose name seems to be a variant spelling of the English word *quit*, is a tycoon and a member of an international cartel. Carl Weber calls Quitt "the last Romantic hero of the business world" (Bly, 83). The reasons behind Quitt's suicide at the end of the play are the focal point of Handke's capitalist tragedy. What happens to Quitt as an individual occurs within the framework and setting of a big city resembling Manhattan. The city, of course, is not specifically New York but could easily be London, Frankfurt or Paris. It is a metropolitan city of the present and of the future (*Unvernünftigen*, 7).

In a newspaper interview with the critic Christian Schulz-Gerstein, Handke stressed the analogy between his working concept of *Unvernünftigen* as a capitalist tragedy and the social structures of betrayal, rejected love, and impotence in Shakespearean theater.[30] Modern-day capitalists, said Handke, can be viewed as the counterparts of those men who commit high treason in Shakespeare's tragedies. In the twentieth century, Handke notes, the love of profit has replaced Elizabethan eroticism. Sublime passion has changed into crassness and manipulation. As a contemporary work, *Unvernünftigen* is a parody of traditional tragedy and depicts emotional crisis over factual details that intentionally mirror modern society's obsession with financial balances, checkbooks, and money-making. The central conflict in the play, however, is also a personal one: the gradual "death" of Hermann Quitt as Handke's symbol of "irrationality" within the rational, capitalist context of modern economics. As a further complication to the theme, *Unvernünftigen* also examines the use of subjectivity, veracity, and especially "poetic thought" as tools of the irrational (life-saving) forces that Quitt tries to employ against the programmatic business world.[31]

Surrounding Quitt are members of his business cartel, all of them symbols of free enterprise: Koerber-Kent, a businessman-priest; Von Wullnow, a symbol of conservative business practice; Paula Tax, a Marxist businesswoman; and Lutz. Each acts according to his or her own principles and is a target of Handke's analysis of corrupt capitalism. A point of conflict among Quitt's friends is their suspicion of him as an erratic business person, never to be entirely trusted. Functioning on the outer rim of this circle is Quitt's wife, truly a "victim" of the capitalist system. Hans, Quitt's confidant and servant, dreams of being rich and enjoying the "freedom" that money can bring him. He is preparing to learn from Quitt's success and would like to have similar social status. Like the minority stockholder Kilb, whose role in the play recalls the wise fool of popular theatrical tradition, Hans's destiny is not without interest. Kilb, on the other hand, is only tolerated by Quitt and his group. His lines are humorous and function as a commentary on the play's picture of corrupt and venal business activity. At the end of the play he is literally strangled in a deadly (comic) embrace by Quitt. Hans, on the other hand, as a symbol of opportunistic social mobility, is a survivor of the "tragedy" that ends Quitt's life. Hans's last words before he exits the stage are significant: "somebody" read his palm and predicted he would change the world. That he will never do so is only ironically evident (*Unvernünftigen*, 95).

The plot of *Unvernünftigen* is simple. In act 1 Quitt forms a cartel with his business associates. The central idea behind the need for the cartel is Quitt's own: he believes that fighting against one another is pointless; as a cartel they can force lesser businesses into bankruptcy (*Unvernünftigen*, 186). Quitt then enumerates the reasons he and his friends must form a cartel: there are too many products on the market, being sold by too many manufacturers, and the ideal capitalist way is to place consumer demand in the hands of a cartel acting as one manufacturing unit. Quitt also has plans to lower workers' wages (*Unvernünftigen*, 28).

In a perceptive analysis of the play, Joseph Federico shows the ambiguity behind Quitt's proposed plan and refers to his role "as the hapless victim of powerful manipulatory forces beyond his control."[32] As a businessman, Quitt has rational insight into the strategies of the business world, but his insight is countermanded by his quixotic sense of personal outrage at common business practices that drive the average business person into "the forest" to feel human (*Unvernünftigen*, 29). If it is true that Quitt's feelings about himself are often expressed in terms of poetic impulses, then it is possible to say, as Federico does (187), that what happens in the play is often the result of its central metaphorical style. In the narrative evolution of the play Quitt is a chief figure, first as a capitalist and then as a figure longing for simplicity and "natural" behavior. For example, his relationship with Hans, with whom he meets daily, is similar to that of Puntila and Matti in Brecht's play *Herr Puntila und sein Knecht Matti* (1940-41). Matti, Puntila's servant and friend, must endure the effects of Puntila's change from kindness to brutality whenever he becomes drunk. Matti walks out on Puntila as a justified act of independence. During an opening scene of *Unvernünftigen* Quitt relates to Hans his "sadness" when he saw his wife in her dressing gown and her "lacquered" toes, a feeling of genuine loneliness, "objective" and yet otherworldly (*Unvernünftigen*, 7).

It is, however, characteristic of Quitt that he should waver between fact and sentiment. As a man in conflict with himself, Quitt's search for unity between those two forces is actually a romantic twist. This is a new element in Handke's work, and it foreshadows related subjective and poetic themes in his subsequent novels. An important aspect of conflict in the play, for example, is the opposition of the language of poetic diction and irrationality to the sterile, nonexpressive language of business and rationality. Whenever Quitt leaves the linguistic jargon of business language and moves toward his inner self, his language changes, too – toward poetic diction, language marked by directness, memory, intimacy, and subjectivity. The richness of this expression is tapped briefly in a short exchange at the end of act 1 when Quitt, in a moment of emotional directness, asks Hans about his life (i.e., his "story"). Hans refuses to believe that Quitt is truly interested and says that the "real" subject of the inquiry is Quitt himself (*Unvernünftigen*, 49).

Poetic diction and irrationality represent for Quitt (and Handke) personal freedom and individuality, the assertion of the inner self and its growth in the romantic sense of limitless expansion. In a speech delivered in 1973 before the Academy of Language and Literature in Darmstadt on the occasion of receiving a literary award, Handke surprised his audience by offering poetic, irrational thought as an alternative to the brute display of economic and political force in today's world.[33] For Handke, however, one's level of language is always directly expressive of one's thought. The Darmstadt speech relates the function of language to either power politics or poetry, and Handke chooses poetry. Handke's speech and Quitt's language in *Unvernünftigen* both make the same distinction between the regenerative language of "poetic thought" and the destructive language of "rational thought." For these reasons, Quitt desires to be "poetic" or irrational. At the end of act 1 Handke sets before his hero the possibility of another kind of existence, the poetic world. The healing vision of this world might be a way out of Quitt's materialistic universe.

Nevertheless, the very end of the first act continues to test Quitt's vulnerability to the seductive forces of economics and technocracy. At a decisive point in the play Quitt is in a pensive mood as he sits listening to Hans's reading passages from a story by the mid-nineteenth-century Austrian novelist Adalbert Stifter. These passages describe an old man's grief and regret at the next day's departure of his younger relative. He mentions the specter of life's failed opportunities. Stifter's flowing mid-nineteenth-century style acts briefly as a narcotic on Quitt as he hears the wisdom of the text: the older man's words about old age and the onset of time and life's lost opportunities (*Unvernünftigen*, 51-53).

If Quitt is perceptive and recognizes the affinity between the truth of Stifter's text and his present self, he is still skeptical of Stifter and his immediate reaction is to call him a nineteenth-century "restorer," a writer who was still capable in his time of creating the illusion that what was being written was credible and attainable (*Unvernünftigen*, 53-54). Contrasting himself with Stifter, a spokesman in nineteenth-century social and literary communities, Quitt says that all *he* ever does is "quote" (use words without meaning) and that authentic signs of life from himself "slip out" purely by accident. Further, a fundamental difference between the two is that Stifter could still convince his audience that his writerly illusions rang true, while Quitt, on the other hand, must play a role that does not even exist. This is a crucial admission in the play, and Quitt decides to abandon his plans for the business cartel, for reasons that have much to do with self-preservation. Linstead notes correctly that Quitt's latest decision has a double function: the Stifter passage gives him insight into himself, but his decision to return to the businessman-rationalist role means that he is unable to escape his identity as a capitalist (1988, 146). His decision to act will prove wrong and bring on his death, thus ending his quest for happiness.

The second act of *Unvernünftigen* develops the disastrous consequences of Quitt's decision. On the stage are several artifacts, a shrinking balloon and a gray boulder among them. The stone is covered with clichéd statements from philosophy and business: "Our greatest sin – The impatience of concepts – The worst is over – The last hope" (*Unvernünftigen*, 57). One can read these words as linguistic signs that point to further entanglements for Quitt. First of all, Hans and Quitt resume their relationship on a more antagonistic level. Quitt says to Hans that he will always remain a servant and that he will only ever dream of becoming a capitalist (*Unvernünftigen*, 57). Dreams, Hans responds, are a key to a better life. Through these words, with a tone of bitterness directed at Quitt, Hans reminds Quitt that money is the true realm of the rich and that poetry belongs to the poor. Quitt next has an encounter with members of the cartel, who try to resume the pact that he has abandoned. They wish to minimize their financial losses. Rhetorical manipulation, clever appeals by Paula Tax to Quitt's sexuality, and an attempt by Kilb to kill Quitt all fail to turn him around, to bring him back to the old way of working for the interests of his group. Kilb is murdered by Quitt, but this act, too, is only a gesture of impotence. Quitt commits suicide when he runs his head against the block of gray stone. His suicide can be overtly attributed to his inability to break out of his role as a businessman and into that of a "poet" within the context of capitalism.

Linstead, however, has pointed out that Quitt's suicide is a parody of the idea of tragedy in that the conflict in which Quitt purports to find himself is a false one. Quitt can thus be seen as the creator of the social and personal conditions under which he suffers, and "such is the all-pervading nature of this role and its effects upon

[Quitt's] inner world that any resistance to it takes on the ambiguous value of also being an extension of it" (1988, 148).

One could also say that Handke himself is not convinced that Quitt's conflict is a real one, since parody is evident throughout the play. The play shows that within the present-day conditions of capitalism, a figure like Quitt can try to escape his role as a capitalist but has no alternative but suicide. He becomes his own victim. Quitt as a capitalist and Quitt as a would-be poet are finally the product of the same phenomenon, capitalism. The death of Quitt, who wants to speak about himself "without using categories," brings on the last category – the lines of an obituary in the next day's newspaper. In this sense, *Unvernünftigen* can be viewed as portraying "truthfully the conditions of modernism which . . . [Handke] sees as a nearly unbridgeable schism between the individual and the world."[34] In this schism, the meaning and the nonmeaning of language are defined by Handke in a new way, within the capitalist setting of contemporary society.

Chapter Three

A Writer's Apprenticeship

Toward a Literary Theory

Peter Handke's earliest prose writings relate to his years as a law student at Graz University during 1961-1965. Alfred Holzinger, then head of Austrian Radio Steiermark, states: "I was able to meet Handke in 1963, when a manuscript of his was sent to me by the poet Alois Hergouth, director of the literary section of *Forum Stadtpark*" (183). Forum Stadtpark and its house journal, *manuskripte*, were a meeting place and a working space for the arts, organized and founded by Graz students and writers. The Graz Group (Grazer Gruppe), which Handke joined soon after his arrival in the city, fostered the revival of post–World War II Austrian literature. It was the successor to an earlier circle of poets and artists – H. C. Artmann, Gerhard Ruhm, and others – headquartered in Vienna. The Vienna Group (Wiener Gruppe), as the earlier circle called themselves, supported a critical, avant-garde attitude toward language, especially poetry. Speaking about the makeup and character of the Graz Group and the content of an early issue of *manuskripte*, Hugh Rorrison notes, "The second issue of *manuskripte* featured the *Wiener Gruppe*, whose pioneering work on language, dialect poetry and drama and concrete poetry as well as their black, anti-bourgeois humor strongly influenced the young Grazer. The "degenerate art" provoked local opposition but the *Forum* weathered the storm with liberal support and *manuskripte* has prospered with the pluralistic, progressive editorial policy" (252).

The first Handke text read by Alfred Holzinger was "Die Überschwemmung" (1867; The Flood), a prose piece that begins with a deliberate artistic strategy: a boy tests the credulity of his blind brother through linguistic ambiguity, conveying either truth or fiction. The reader is also assumed to be "blind" in the sense that he or she also knows very little about the actual state of affairs and must work through the levels of meaning induced by language, into the reality of the setting and the events that enfold: an approaching flood on the banks of the river, where, it turns out, the boys are located. This text, like several of Handke's early prose texts, has no story in the conventional sense, only whatever the reader can garner from the estranged linguistic process. A second prose text from Handke's Graz period, "Über den Tod eines Fremden" (1967; Concerning the death of a stranger), challenges the truth of a tale about the discovery of a man by a youth searching for a ball in the ruins of a bunker. The piece is structured as a "montage of sentences that is possibly the beginning of a narrative, yet this assumption is challenged by the I-narrator himself" (Alfred Holzinger, 184). Here Handke stresses the essential difference between the narrator's subjective reality and the deception offered by another, fictional reality. If this piece claims to assert facts, it can never prove them.

The story "Begrüssing des Aufsichtsrats" (1967; Greetings from the board of directors) is an eccentric elaboration on a key sentence of its text: "The beams are collapsing."[1] A group of stockholders has gathered in an old, weathered farmhouse in the middle of winter to hear the chairman's report on the financial status of their company. The chairman notes repeatedly that he is not interested in political or social implications of business, nor does he desire to deliver a "political" report. The chairman assures his nervous audience that the beams of the house are not collapsing, yet the reader feels that this is not the case. In an exit worthy of Wagnerian grand opera, the last words of the chairman's report are never finished. This event prepares the reader not only for the collapse of the house (reality) but also for the mendacity of language (in the chairman's report). Comedy and absurdity, recalling the black humor of Franz Kafka's parables, unmask the hidden truth as well as the metaphorical relationship between the collapse of the house and the fall of capitalist society.

Handke later incorporated several texts of the Graz period into chapters of his first two novels. They provided, in fact, the titles of those novels: "Die Hornissen" (1963; The Hornets) and "Der Hausierer" (1963; The Peddler). In the Graz "Hornissen" a woman speaks to her children about a sick man in the next room and recalls that he appeared one day with his father, an army deserter sought by the police (i.e., the hornets). The woman's father gave the deserter shelter. The sick man's memories, in turn, blend with the memories of the woman. Only several pages long, the text is a display piece of Faulknerian memory within a context that recalls key events of the past. In "Hausierer" the author contrasts the shifting meaning of the word *peddler* in different contexts, first in a prosaic film episode, and then in a stage play. This changing perspective is a demonstration of Wittgenstein's thesis that the meaning of a word lies uniquely in its use.

The text "Das Standrecht" (1967; Martial law) has been the subject of extended critical commentary. In the 1967 essay "Ich bin ein Bewohner des Elfenbeinturms" (I am a dweller in an ivory tower) Handke reveals that "Das Standrecht" is based on his reading of an actual legal text denoting those procedures to be undertaken by civil authorities in the event of an uprising among citizens and the subsequent reestablishment of social order, including the trial and execution of the perpetrators responsible for the rebellion and social disruption. Handke notes his initial reaction to this original text, specifically to a reference to the "guilty" verdict: "The theoretical language of the legal text did not seem to refer to a concrete instance of death, but it showed me a new way to look at the phenomenon of dying and death. The legal text changed my earlier habits of thinking about the presentation of death and dying in literature. . . . I then decided to write a text that took over the methods of a legal text into literature."[2]

Manfred Mixner, however, emphasizes Handke's language in the reworked text, noting that it is language that demonstrates flexibility in depicting fear and anxiety. Words are used as functional devices, setting the stage for a "possible rebellion" or even the "possible" event of an "execution" of men responsible for the overthrowing of government. Handke, according to Mixner, has written a political text showing how government can manipulate language to create fear and terror among those contemplating any opposition to established authority.[3] To Linstead, however, "Das Standrecht" departs at its midpoint from a successful emulation of legalistic jargon and moves toward an "esthetic" exploration of that language, adopting a mode of satire and thus offering the reader a clear instance of the author's "esthetically organizing, seemingly fixed, unhappy brutal reality" (1988, 38). "Das Standrecht" serves to demonstrate that in

his Graz period, young Handke was not only an avid revisionist of
literary forms, even those beyond the scope of traditional literature;
he was also a determined inventor of literary methodology that func-
tioned to estrange the reality of language, whether it came from literature or not.

Through economic necessity, young Handke was induced to
expand his literary activity at the Graz radio station. Alfred Holzinger
gave him an opportunity to write occasional pieces (*feuilletons*) on
an assortment of topics drawn from the emerging pop culture of the
1960s: the music of the Beatles; American feature films and cartoons;
the circus; popular fiction (*Trivialliteratur*). He was paid by the
word and was limited to how much he might earn for a piece:
"Pieces that were fifteen minutes long got 300 Schillings. I could
have done more but I had to stop after a certain number of sentences" (*Bewohner*, 7). Handke also reviewed books, and on Sunday
afternoons he dramatized classical novels for his audience. He produced a 14-episode reading of Dostoyevski's *Crime and Punishment*
that featured his wife, the stage actress Libgart Schwarz, in the leading role of Sonia (Holzinger, 193). Six additional prose texts, all of
which found their way into the 1967 short story collection *Begrüssung des Aufsichtsrats*, were written and then read on the radio at
this time. Among them were "Prüfungsfrage I" (Test question I) and
"Prüfungsfrage II" (Test question II), a pair of anecdotes with unexpected, absurdist conclusions, typical of the short prose pieces
formulated by the German nineteenth-century master storyteller
Heinrich von Kleist. Both anecdotes stress the inexorable course of
the law. In the first, a father enters a church to pray for help to feed
his starving children. He finds some money, but after this good
fortune he is convicted of hiding the source of his sudden wealth. In
the second "Prüfungsfrage," a father playing with his child throws
him into the air. The child dies on his return fall, and the father is
charged with murder. To demonstrate his innocence, the father
decides to repeat the act with his second child, who falls dead, too.
Handke's two texts, in their brevity, reveal their moral and ethical
ambiguity quickly and efficiently. As one reads these anecdotes,
along with their companion piece, a "sober," unadorned synopsis of
Kafka's novel *Der Prozess* (1925; The Trial) – Handke uses the same
title – one realizes that Handke's reworking of classical literature is
another instance of literary deconstruction and defamiliarization of

their genres for the contemporary reader. Handke's version of *The Trial*, for example, reduces Kafka's novel to its essentials: the recounting of specific details from its plot, following "K" through the stages of his inquiry into the source and nature of his guilt. The new text is free of metaphor, symbols, and redundant description. As in his Kleist-like pieces, Handke refuses to emulate the rambling style of literary narration. He demands clarity and avoids discursive language.

The fledgling author decided to leave Graz and the university by the end of the summer semester in 1966 (Alfred Holzinger, 196). His creative achievements at Graz were steering him away from legal studies. He had published pieces in *manuskripte*. In the late winter of 1965 he had tendered a typewritten copy of his first language piece, *Publikumsbeschimpfung*, to Holzinger, soliciting an opinion on its viability as a stage play. His first novel, *Die Hornissen*, had already been accepted (with the help of intermediaries) by the prestigious publisher Suhrkamp, a West German house, for its new authors' listing and subsequent publication. In April 1966 Handke made his notorious protest at Princeton about the miserable state of modern German prose before the members of Group 47. Handke used the pejorative term *Beschreibungsimpotenz* (impotent description) to label that group's prototypical approach to realistic writing. This sweeping generalization was both seductive in its breadth and destructive. He later withdrew the term in a generous apology (*Bewohner*, 29). Handke had meant to "correct" the erroneous impression held by realist writers of fiction that the objects of realism, related in writing, were identical with the processes of reality itself. Such writing was therefore "impotent." Though Handke paid dearly for his impertinence in daring to attack the alleged "realism" of German post–World War II writers like Günter Grass, Uwe Johnson, and Peter Weiss, who had earned worldwide laurels among readers and critics, he chose to explain himself in print. At Princeton he read excerpts from his second novel-in-progress, *Der Hausierer*. His life as a young writer in Graz had given him the exhilarating freedom to criticize what he deplored as a false and unauthentic approach to language and descriptive realism. Because he had undergone an apprenticeship in Graz as an aspirant to literary fame, been published as an author, and established a radio audience, Handke was not exactly the unknown figure he was inferred to be

when news came back to the European literary establishment about
his speech at Princeton. Dieter Zimmer, a reporter for *Die Zeit*, in a
detailed analysis of the events at Princeton, notes that Handke was
not very articulate in his criticism, yet to Zimmer's surprise, he
received "a brotherly kiss" from those who might have known
better.[4]

Graz, Alfred Holzinger maintains, delineates the beginnings of
Handke's literary achievement and establishes the continuity
between his origins and his later, mature development as a
spokesman for postmodernist German literature (196). His early
writings and radio activity adumbrate themes and announce stylistic
and literary devices found in the *Sprechstücke* of Handke's theater
and novels, such as *Die Hornissen, Der Hausierer,* and *Die Angst
des Tormanns beim Elfmeter.* In the early short prose texts, literary
genres and models of writing were deconstructed – that is, cast
anew as writerly vehicles for the transmission of another underlying
reality of social and esthetic importance.

An essay Handke wrote in 1966 is pivotal for understanding the
development of his literary theory. "Zur Tagung der Gruppe 47"
(Group 47 meets in the USA) expounds the substance of Handke's
charge against the group assembled at Princeton.[5] These writers,
Handke asserts, are using "dead" words as a literary medium. A
"dead" word for Handke is one that has no definite signification.
Such writing only adds to the sheer number of words found in the
pages of any text of realistic literature. Writers must learn to focus
their efforts on reflective language, the stuff of which literature is
composed. Handke says, "I have nothing against description.
Description is a necessary means of arriving at reflection. I support
description but not the kind of description practiced in today's Germany under the name of 'realism.' . . . People forget that literature is
made with words of a language, and not with things described by
language. . . . Words for objects are taken for the objects themselves"
("Tagung," 29-30). Handke adds that the language of contemporary
German realistic literature functions like a "lens," allowing the
reader only to "recognize" rather than "see" an object. For Handke,
seeing means perception and reflection (consciousness) in the
reader's encounter with the written word. He advocates the shat-
tering of all glasslike language.

Another issue brought up by Handke at the Princeton meeting was the tendency of literary criticism to judge writers on the basis of their commitment to social and political realism. This judgment by critics, Handke observed, is one related to the "specificity" or "reality" of the world depicted in their writing. Handke articulates his firm stand against politically committed literature in "Tagung": the concept of an ideological literature is a contradiction in terms, "ideology" being a creature of pamphleteering, not literature (31).

"Die Literatur ist romantisch" (1966; Literature is romantic) is a clever and well-reasoned essay against Group 47's support of political and social literature.[6] This essay's many topical headings are set off in the lefthand margin. The central issues discussed are (a) What writer is *not* committed? (*engagiert*); (b) a committed writer, however, has a political agenda; (c) to be truly committed is to act; (d) the worldview of a committed writer is indeed a utopian one; and

(e) Is the term *commitment* proper for literature? Handke devotes a major portion of the essay to criticism of Jean-Paul Sartre's distinction between the writer (*Schriftsteller*) and the poet (*Dichter*). For Sartre, the writer is committed; he unmasks contemporary reality and is interested in changing it. For Sartre, the writer, Handke says, makes a decision to "show" the nature of a human being to another human being. Handke challenges Sartre's assertions that the poet's only realm is literature and that poetic language is an antiquated inheritance of the nineteenth century. Not only does Handke express his anger at Sartre's implication that the writer has a higher function than the poet – for the writer is a symbol of *littérature engagée* – but that a writer is the sole productive representative of change-inducing literature. Handke's answer to Sartre is succinctly argued: "There is no 'committed' literature. The concept is a contradictory one. There are committed human beings, but no committed writers. The word *committed* is a political one. At the most it can refer to political writers, who, however, are not writers in the sense that interests us here, but they are rather politicians, who are writing what they want to say. Who can name a literary work of Sartre's that, according to his own definition is not committed literature? Who could name a work of Sartre's in which words are only activity and not a will toward a literary style?" ("Literatur," 43).

Handke's argument against Sartre's line of reasoning is well taken, since his own books interweave politics and philosophy and cross the border between works of a creative writer (the poet) and those of a *littérature engagée* (the writer). Using Sartre as an example, Handke refuses to accept the idea of thesis-oriented literature and its medium, the politically committed novelist. Further refuting the possibility of "committed literature," Handke asserts that art and literature have no specific meaning other than that which defines their own esthetic necessity: "The essence of art is neither singular nor pluralistic. It has neither countable nor tangible meanings. The meaning of art is explainable only with the 'words' of art itself, while political commitment is describable with other words, from [the outer realm of politics]. . . . Commitment is materially influenced, while literature is formalistic. Change the form [the genre] of literature and you change its essence" ("Literatur," 43-44).

Another hortatory, programmatic essay in young Handke's arsenal against realistic and political literature is "Ich bin ein Bewohner des Elfenbeinturms." This essay is important for several reasons: (a) it defines the reading of literature as a learning experience equal to an academic education; (b) it defends the function of literature as a critical means for the evaluation of reality, involving perception and reflection; (c) it emphasizes the role of literary method in the writing of literature; and (d) it relates the renewal of literary method to the renewal of consciousness for the reader. In the essay Handke alternates between his roles as a reader of literature and a writer, the creator of a literary text. The essay opens with his tribute to literature as his great educator: "For a long time, literature has been the means of my having learned more about myself. It has helped me to recognize that I existed, that I was in the world" ("Bewohner," 19). And in the same confessional mode Handke admits that literature was his liberation from guilt and "sickness," by which he means the social and spiritual inheritance of his time and place. Here it is helpful to remember that Handke matriculated as a student in a Catholic institution, submitting defiantly to the protracted regimen of the Church. Literature and reading led him toward "true" consciousness, away from self-absorption. He learned that his "abnormality" was a part of normal human growth and development. Yet a perceptive reader of Handke will realize that his continuing preoccupation with literary "models" and "methods" is surely a remnant of his disciplined Catholic education, brief as it was, as well as of his legal studies in Graz.

In "Bewohner," Handke, always an opponent of prescribed education, attributes to literature new possibilities of seeing, speaking, thinking and existing. His true education, he says, came from the books of writers like Heinrich von Kleist, Gustave Flaubert, Franz Kafka, William Faulkner, and Alain Robbe-Grillet. In later essays he names other authors (Adalbert Stifter, Goethe, Friedrich Hölderlin) from whom he learned that books can change the lives of others, since they had changed his own.

Shifting his critical perspective from that of a reader to that of an author, Handke says, "Now, as an author, the familiar ways of describing the world no longer satisfy me" ("Bewohner," 20). Handke states a strong case for renewing literary methods and literary genres: "I use a literary method only once. To use it again is impossible. Used twice, a literary genre [in German: *Modell der Darstellung*] has nothing new to offer, at the most only a variation of what has been used before. A literary genre, used for the first time to depict reality, can be realism, but the second time it becomes a 'mannerism,' is unreal, even though it might be called realism by others" ("Bewohner," 20).

In the passage above, *Modell* is roughly equivalent to "genre" or an "ideal" literary form. Handke's early literary texts, as one notes, use traditional literary genres didactically and instructively, reworking and deconstructing them to the point where they emerge with a different esthetic structure. Handke thus believes that writing "successful" literature is always a question of finding both a right genre model and a correct method, of deliberately choosing a reflective literary method that enables the reader to "see" the world anew.[7] Handke's most convincing argument against recycled literary method, however, lies in his related point that familiar literary methodology reproduces a world of lifeless imagery. An uninventive writer will thus fail to challenge the esthetic and ontological perceptions of the reader, and the reader will respond in kind: "When the method is 'worn out,' that is to say, when the method has become 'natural,' the most trivial and familiar things become a mannerism. . . . Content acquires a fixed meaning and is repeated again" ("Bewohner," 21-22).

Young Handke's esthetic and theoretical platform for the renewal of literature has theoretical parallels to the program of literary renewal advocated by two leading practitioners of *le nouveau roman* (the new novel), French novelists Alain Robbe-Grillet and Nathalie Sarraute.[8] The three essays discussed thus far – "Die Literatur ist romantisch," "Zur Tagung der Gruppe 47," and "Ich bin ein Bewohner des Elfenbeinturms" – were in fact published after Robbe-Grillet's *Pour un nouveau roman* (1962; For a new novel) and Sarraute's (*L'ère du soupcon* (1956; The Age of suspicion).[9] All three writers adopt a polemical, well-reasoned defense of the new novel, using arguments in defining reality, literary description, the methodology of the novel, and artistic "commitment." For Sarraute, as for Handke, an author is also a reader, both the creator and the receiver of the literary text, for whom "a story told in the first person satisfies the legitimate scruples of the author. In addition, [such a story] has the appearance . . . of real experience and authenticity, which impresses the reader and dispels his mistrust" (66). The honest writer, Sarraute further notes, writes about himself, ignoring the "story" (Handke's word is *Geschichte*); her remarks parallel Handke's in "Bewohner": "As an author, I am not interested in either showing or conquering reality. My main business is my own reality" (25). Sarraute and Handke agree that the contemporary reader and the author do not believe one another, and that this underlying mistrust (in an "age of suspicion") impels them both to work for change in the novel.

On the other hand, Robbe-Grillet's 1963 essay "Time and Description in Fiction Today," the subject of which is the changed role of time and description in the new novel, sheds further light on Handke's 1966 attack on contemporary German realism at Princeton. For young Handke, the difference between facile, "impotent description" and its opposite is the difference between words that mirror objects and those that "see" – that is, that recognize familiar objects and see them anew within a context of estrangement. This estrangement for Handke is tantamount to writerly creativity and enhancement of the reading experience. Robbe-Grillet's essay reveals a possible source for Handke's ideas: "Description once claimed to reproduce a pre-existing reality; it now asserts its creative function. . . . It once made us see things, now it seems to destroy them, as if its intention to discuss them aimed only at blurring their contours, at making them incomprehensible, at causing them to disappear altogether" (147).

The "creativity" and "destruction" brought about by a successful writerly description of the objects of the real world, so often alluded to in the critical remarks of Robbe-Grillet, are linked by him to the renewal of literary method for each text by the novelist. Thus description, according to Robbe-Grillet, is created ever anew in fiction, within a context in which "the real, the false, and illusion become more or less the subject of all modern works" (150).

Experimental Fiction, 1966-1972

Die Hornissen

Die Hornissen (1966; The Hornets), Peter Handke's first novel, remains untranslated into English, but a rudimentary acquaintance with this important text is essential for an understanding of Handke's beginnings as a novelist, especially in its apparent debt to the structuralist theory and criticism of Roland Barthes.[10] Handke has acknowledged Barthes's influence on both *Die Hornissen* and *Der Hausierer*, as he noted in a 1979 interview with June Schlueter: "[Reading Barthes] was important for me fifteen years ago, for structures. It helped me to see structures, and that is a pleasure, because there is formlessness in every phenomenon, everything for itself, and all are confused. It helped me at that time to see an order, not an hierarchical order but a structural order" (1981, 173-74). If Handke suggests here that he later moved away from structuralism as a theoretical basis for writing fiction, these remarks on the origins of his esthetics are nevertheless interesting and merit attention, since structuralism still survives as a creative force in his latest fiction (*Der Chinese des Schmerzes, Die Wiederholung*). Below the surface of *Hornissen* – whose impenetrability of meaning and composition has eluded critics (there is very little criticism of the text in German and English) – can be found the bones of a structuralist novel, devoid of conventional narrative and description.[11] Since there is no one way of reading *Hornissen* that accommodates all the important aspects of the text, my own discussion will be a composite of those critical sources that I feel offer insightful interpretations. These sources address the primary issues of narrative reconstruction, narrative

point of view, autobiographical detail, and structuralist analysis. The
last issue links Handke more specifically to Barthes and suggests to
the reader not only how the text might be read "as a unit" but even
how Handke functions as a structuralist writer in his first novel.

A prime reason for the novel's reputation as an inaccessible
work lies in its mosaiclike dispersal of narrative elements and
episodes. The problems this creates for the reader, should he or she
even try to reconstruct a connected narrative, are real and seem to
have been anticipated by the German publisher Rowohlt, who, in a
brief introductory statement, offers a précis of "narrative highlights."
This summary, not found in the Suhrkamp edition, has often been
quoted by critics as a guide to the reader and even used as a point of
departure for their own interpretations of the novel's narrative
development. The précis, quoted below, is helpful as a general
statement about the author's intentions, especially about the shape
of the narrative's trajectory within a prose equivalent of a hall of
mirrors:

> Die Hornissen is an attempt to describe the origins of a novel. A man read a
> book many years ago; or he did not even read it but he was told its story by
> someone else. Now, however, on a summer's day, whether it be a coincidence
> deriving from a confluence of events occurring within himself and to the blind
> hero of the book, he is reminded again of the disappeared book, which he
> thought he had read. The man reconstructs [a mental equivalent] of the novel
> from broken "pieces" he believes he remembers; from words from sentences;
> from half-lost images – all this happens in such a way that it is impossible to
> determine whether what happens occurs in the new novel or to the hero of
> the old one, or even to the man itself. This "new novel" is Die Hornissen.

Hornissen is not structured in conventional chapters but contains approximately 67 units or freestanding parts of various lengths,
each one of which features words, sentences, and images that focus
on a specific aspect of the novel. These units follow no special order,
whether of time, narrative, or point of view. The novel's primary narrator is Gregor Benedikt, a blind man introduced in an early section
called "Das Einsetzen der Erinnerung" (The Beginning of memory).
Gregor, an older man in the opening pages of the text, is recalling
events surrounding a key episode of the past – the onset of his
blindness on a day when, as a younger man, he was searching for his
missing brother Hans. A third brother, Matt, had drowned earlier

while in the company of Hans. Yet it is never entirely clear, because of Handke's disjointed narrative construction, whether Gregor's remembrances of that day come from a novel he read long ago or from actual events of his life. Throughout Handke's book, the evolving memory of the narrator, as he struggles to separate fact from fiction, is analogous to that of Handke's reader, who is obliged to see, perceive, remember, and think in the same ways the blind narrator uses. It is thus impossible for a reader to know with precision on which level of narrative he or she should function. With this dilemma in mind, David Darby has written on the receding content of the "forgotten" novel in the mind of Gregor. If there was originally a novel for Gregor to remember, he could only forget it as time went on, since Gregor, along with the reader, is involved in a "compound reading process involving both attrition and the addition of new elements," and this process forever excludes anyone's definitive access to an immutable text, whether for Gregor or the reader (259). An apparently simple act of reading becomes a hurdle for all concerned.

Another problem in reading the novel is the narrative point of view. It is only at the end of *Hornissen*, in a section called "Die Enstehung der Geschichte" (The Origin of the story), that the reader is introduced to the voice of a second narrator who, as another narrator, purports to relate objectively the background of preceding events (*Hornissen*, 271). This turns out to be a retelling of narrative highlights without Gregor's estranging sense of blindness. The second narrator disavows blindness as a factor in the first narrator's recalling of past and present events, intimating that Gregor is a liar. He says that "what [Gregor] wants to see, he does indeed see; whenever he wants, he has a second face, from which a far-off distance becomes visible" (*Hornissen*, 274). The first narrator, says the second, is content to "think out" what can be thought out (*ausdenken*), and he accepts that as the truth. Certainly Gregor is never far from thought or even the processes of thought. The sense of blindness, as well as the activity of thought, triggers outstanding units of narration in *Hornissen*. Since Gregor is blind, he can hear well, and his developed sense of hearing is an aid to remembering sounds and places of the past and present. Fear and dreams, the reconstruction within Gregor's mind of a long tale centering on the longed-for return of his brother Hans, "Der Mann mit dem Seesack"

(The Man with a duffel bag), are literary devices and a narrative episode initiated by Gregor's dependency on sound. The novel's longest section, "Der Heimgang" (The Way home), is a display piece of memory, especially of stages in the movement of memory. The blind narrator in this section reconstructs what he believes to be true about the events of that fateful day: Hans's disappearance and his own subsequent blindness. Thought functions here also as an act of reconciliation and understanding. As the narrator returns home, he comes to the practical end of his efforts to reconstruct exact details of memory. Handke now ends his novel – that is, that portion of the novel which relates to the positioning of Gregor Benedikt's point of view in the narrative.

Involuntary memory, narrative, and narration are thus linked as essential components around which interpretation and meaning in *Hornissen* must revolve. Handke's book, however, also relies on autobiographical details culled from his early life. Thomas Barry claims that, in this sense, the text, despite its obvious experiments with narration, fits into a "kind of existential estheticism; personal journeys of self-exploration and self-definition, in which art and the imagination provide a temporary means of transcendence for [the author's] estranged consciousness" (1983, 197). Hans Widrich has noted, on the other hand, that the precision of place description in *Hornissen* makes it possible for a reader to follow the setting and "uncover" the realistic background against which Gregor Benedikt not only moves through past and present but recalls them through an act of memory.[12] In his article, which articulates the actual setting and places in *Hornissen*, linking the novel's text to the geography and history of Altenmarkt, Handke's birthplace, Widrich cites two facts. First, the blind narrator's comment that his blindness occurred at a time when "bombers flew in the night" refers to World War II, when bombers not only flew over Altenmarkt but dropped bombs too. The novel, however, never specifically cites bombing as a direct cause of Gregor's blindness. Second, Gregor is functioning within the framework of Handke's own dualistic cultural experience as a Slovene-Austrian (Fellinger, 26-27). The reader notes that the church where Gregor and his brothers attend Sunday Mass is a Slovene congregation, since signs for the Stations of the Cross are written in that language. An especially autobiographical detail, however, lies in Handke's decision to join together in this episode two common but

disparate images of village life: the solemnity of the sacrifice symbolized in the death of the Lamb of God, and the village ritual, as
Handke remembers it, of killing a pig. Both events flow together dis-
passionately in a section of the text entitled "Die Liturgie" (The
Liturgy). The church congregation, Handke notes ironically, is more
"passive" during the stylized enactment of the church ritual
(*Hornissen*, 111).

Sundry other details of his past life in Altenmarkt, before Handke
began to write his novel in 1963, locate the text in historical time
amid particular details that would satisfy an Austrian village archivist.
In one episode Gregor's father is busy cutting reeds, a favorite food
for farm animals (part 4); in another, a horse suffers from flies (part
10). Today, notes Widrich, farmers in Griffen and Altenmarkt have
tractors instead of horses to plow the land (Fellinger, 31). There are
no cars in *Hornissen*; Gregor's family is too poor to own one, so
Gregor often asks whether the milkman's truck has arrived, in the
hope that he catch a ride into town. The milkman of Handke's youth
would pick up both empty milk containers and passengers too poor
to keep a car or even a bicycle. Those lacking the money to buy a
bicycle, however, could ride a bus, something that the blind Gregor
tries to do. About the role of transportation in the novel and its
relation to Handke, Widrich observes, "Twenty years ago . . . hardly
anyone had his own car. People rode the bus, that today as then,
went to the nearest towns or cities – up to Klagenfurt or in the other
direction, up to Graz. The young law student Handke used the bus"
(Fellinger, 32).

Since the blind narrator in *Hornissen* fails in his efforts to reconstruct possible details of the "lost novel," or even the exact details of
the onset of his blindness, he will never uncover the facts surrounding the fate of his missing brother Hans. Gregor's quest for a
"reading" of the novel via searching within himself is never directly
linked to the reader's "reading" events in Gregor's past. Handke's
final image in the novel of the remembering first narrator is that of a
man who must settle for a tentative sense of the truth. Gregor's
blindness is finally a physical barrier as real as the difference
between night and day. Night is a metaphor here not only for the
narrator's blindness but also for the dead end of memory. In the
meantime, however, Handke's own book evolves, under its unique
laws of composition and meaning, within the reader's imagination, a

structuralist process as defined by Roland Barthes.[13] *Hornissen* gives
the reader ample demonstration of Handke's critical precept that
perception and thought are structured aspects of human experience.
If a reading of Handke's text leaves one with the lingering sense that
Hornissen "is a narrative about the construction of a narrative, its
subject matter . . . in large part the description of its composition,"
then one must acknowledge that structuralist technique, specifically
the technique of making a novel, is Handke's prime concern (Darby,
261). In his text technique and structure relate not only to esthetic
creation but to structuralist activity as well. *Hornissen* deconstructs
both its own text and the genre of the traditional novel, with its conventional narrative, strict point of view, and chronological time. As a
structuralist novelist, Handke proceeds in such a way that his novel
makes manifest the rules under which a conventional novel
functions.

The esthetic pleasure for the reader of *Hornissen* lies, as I have
indicated, in perceiving how the book conveys meaning or nonmeaning within the following areas: (a) subjective memory, (b) simple narrative, (c) multiple narration, and (d) autobiographical detail.
Handke's novel is dissembled in a way that highlights the importance
or nonimportance of episodes to a reading of the novel. Narrative
meaning in the novel cannot be found apart from the reader's
response to Handke's structuralist sense of narrative order. Handke
has made a special effort to articulate the function of the novel's
episodes in such a way that his novel is uniquely different. What
emerges finally is a new category of the traditional novel. Handke's
structuralist activity in *Hornissen* demonstrates Barthes's observation that a goal "of structuralism is not man endowed with meanings
but man fabricating meanings" (218). Handke is just such a fabrica-
tor who, along with his two narrators and the reader, can in all innocence impose many readings of the book. Handke seems to be wel-
coming this open-ended approach, especially in those parts of the
novel that point to the elusive memory-recall of the blind narrator,
who creates estrangement for whatever is seen, perceived, and felt.
The reader must contend, of course, with the claimed objectivity of
the second narrator. Narrative reconstruction in *Hornissen* is dis-
persed into episodes unrelated by time. Intentional ambiguity, discontinuity, and randomness characterize many parts of the novel
that could serve as ordinary informational units. If Handke's novel is

antinarrative, it does include elements of the author's *petite histoire* (autobiography) as a youth growing up in the austerity and poverty of Altenmarkt. The reader of *Hornissen* must settle for the reading of a mutant text that works against any definitive interpretation and reveals the author as a structuralist "placed under the common sign of what we [can] call structural man, defined not by his ideas or his languages, but by his imagination – in other words, by the way in which he mentally experiences structure" (Barthes, 214).

Der Hausierer

An early reference to the writing of his second novel, *Der Hausierer* (1967; The Peddler), is found at the end of Handke's 1967 "Bewohner" essay, where he advocates a changing methodology of the novel and a renewal of conventional fictional processes: "For the novel that I have just written, I borrowed a genre of existing fiction. I did not invent a story: I found one. I found a plot of the murder mystery, with its representative clichés of murder, death, fright, fear, pursuit, and torture. . . . I realized that these devices were derived from reality, that they had once entailed a realistic literary method. . . . I chose a method that would call attention . . . to an ineffective literary method, so that this older method might once again become nonliterary and perceptive" ("Bewohner," 28).

Since Handke argues that the reader deserves the chance to create the text of his or her own murder mystery, a text relevant to the patterns of the reader's own consciousness, he also assumes that the old scheme of writing a murder mystery has exhausted itself for the writer as well. As the writer of *Der Hausierer*, his primary goal will be to point the way toward new possibilities of "presentation" (*die Darstellung*), to deconstruct the standard methodology of the murder mystery, to uncover a sense of "play," reflection, and sensory experience.[14]

The methodology that Handke chooses for *Hausierer* is, in fact, the chief interest of the book, which remains untranslated into English. *Hausierer* is first and foremost a book demonstrating literary method, not a text of fiction, and more than any other book by Handke it clearly demands a willing reader, especially a reader who brings to the text an innate sense of the content and structure of a genre murder mystery. A consideration of the framework of Handke's book makes the need for this readerly background appar-

ent. Each chapter is divided into first a theoretical and then an expositional (narrative) section. The theoretical framework of a genre
murder mystery underlies the theoretical sections, which are set off
in italics so as to stress their separateness. The narrative sections of
each chapter are intentionally elusive and do not clearly relate to any
one murder mystery the reader might recognize. The words and sentences of the narrative sections consist of probable sentences from
probable mysteries. The time sequence of these sentences is neither
sequential nor chronological, and the reader is frustrated if he or she
tries to identify any one character, including the murderer. At the
end of the novel there is no obvious motivation or even a resolution
of any particular crime.

The reader is forced to rely on the theoretical portion as a guide
to the narrative reading of each chapter. The chapter titles, however,
are specific and developmental. A sampling of seven of the 12 chapter titles includes (a) "The Order before the Disorder," (b) "The
First Disorder," (c) "The Order of the First Disorder," (d)
"Unraveling the First Disorder," (e) "The Investigation," (f) "The
Interrogation," and (g) "The Seeming Return to Order . . . before the
Second Disorder." In the rest of the book the police suspect comes
upon a second murder and is once more interrogated, tortured, and
then set free. He finds the "real" murderer, and everything returns
to normalcy. The banality of everyday life absorbs murder into its
routine, and the reader is invited to enjoy the serenity of an orderly
world: "The murder, scarcely explained, happened so long ago, that
it is no longer true" (*Hausierer*, 201). The last line of the text notes
that children are playing at murder – that is, murder has been
reduced to the level of a child's game.

As the theoretical portions of Handke's novel propose, and as
the narrative sections suggest, the book's dual sections are mutually
dependent. They help the reader penetrate the codependence of
theory and exposition, especially in a genre like the murder mystery,
a literary form that overlaps the boundary line between popular literature and "serious" fiction. Handke makes a unique effort to inject
a deeper vitality into this popular, overused genre of writing. The
murder mystery, Handke believes, is always the continuation of
another story. The source of the first story is never known, and *a*
murder mystery is only a public manifestation of *the* first story. Here
is an example from *Hausierer* of a first story moving into a mystery:

"A man steps onto the street. The cigarette stub rolls over the side-walk." A murder mystery is told from the viewpoint of an outsider, someone from another place. This person in Handke's novel is a peddler, a stranger, who, when he arrives in a new place, is confronted with the spectacle of perfect order; he is a witness to this order (chapter 1). The following example of Handke's expositional writing in the *second* half of the first chapter is typical: the peddler "notes how the order around him turns into a game. The sound of glasses is no threatening sound. Whenever anyone talks to him, he answers with a gesture and a glance. A woman's laughter is absorbed by other sounds. Although the peddler thinks he will never know anyone here, he tries to see the faces around him. . . . The fingers that he thought were drawn together, have opened up. . . . The bucket seems to be empty. The coin is still warm" (*Hausierer*, 15). Order thus precedes disorder, the main "event" of the second chapter. Disorder, however, is Handke's key word in the text for murder. Murder is a disruption of reality, and it gives reality a definite time and place. The peddler unwittingly becomes a witness to murder: "Somewhere someone cries out and a door slams with a threat. A piece of fruit falls out of a man's hand" (*Hausierer*, 33).

The next step in the theoretical development of Handke's genre murder mystery would occur after the discovery of the murder, or the attempt by the police to clarify the reasons and the circumstances of the murder. The reconstruction of these events begins with the moment of the murder, "in which time stands still. . . . Time is divided into before and after. . . . Wrong questions and wrong answers are given" (*Hausierer*, 47). It is at this point, however, that Handke's peddler enters the investigation on his own volition but against his will. He is dissatisfied with the pace of the police inquiry and its emerging conclusions. He is the only one who knows facts that can bring together random details of the inquiry. Like the photographer in Michelangelo Antonioni's 1966 feature film *Blow-up*, whose obsession with detail turns him into a photographer-voyeur and who, in pursuit of detail, "enlarges" it to the point where it finds its place in the total scheme of "the mystery," the peddler has facts that the police do not (chapter 3). The next chapter of *Hausierer* is a demasking of the "order" with which the novel began. The peddler begins an interrogation, door-to-door, among the neighbors of the murder victim. He focuses on objects (*Gegenstände*) with which the

victim was associated. As an outsider in the community, the peddler
is ideally suited to ask the right questions, yet the neighbors resent
his intrusive inquiries: "The obstacles that the peddler meets on the
way to finding the true story, give way to a new one, one that
revolves around the old one" (*Hausierer*, 64). Chapter 5 introduces
other steps of Handke's murder mystery analysis, those "obligatory"
episodes in which the unofficial investigator (the peddler) becomes
the object of pursuit by the true murderer and has a face-to-face
encounter with that nemesis. The peddler, confronted with a "cold
object" at his neck, is "frightened to death" (*Hausierer*, 103).

Since he is a stranger whom the police suspect for his assumed
presence at the scene of the murder, the peddler is interrogated and
then tortured by the police (chapter 6). He is urged to confess whatever he knows. The peddler, however, is more than "the wrong
man" in the hands of police. He becomes the quintessential outsider
who is a victim of cruel police investigation. Power (*Macht*) and
force (*Gewalt*) are key words here. For Handke, those with power
are more to be feared than those with force, since power conveys
the right to use force. The police interrogation episode in *Hausierer*
depicts the relationship between abusive power and force. The peddler is helpless before his interrogators. Handke says, "Giving no
answer will bring on measures. At this point of the murder mystery,
the interrogated person is either in the impersonal power of a law,
or in the illegal power of a person, who can set events into motion.
Law is serving the cause of coercion" (*Hausierer*, 104). The peddler
is released and escapes further questioning only through deception,
but the interrogation has run its course. No more questions can be
asked. The peddler feigns a response through a nonresponse. Only
later does he feel the full horror of what he has endured.

In *Hausierer* Handke is especially careful with his portrayal of
order, disorder, fear, pursuit, and torture as elements of perception
and feeling. He is anxious to liberate those words from the context
of the genre murder mystery. The text of *Hausierer* teaches the
reader how his or her own perceptions (especially fantasies) might
create fear in a supremely active way (Klinkowitz and Knowlton, 22).
Fear in the first police interrogation scene is intended to illuminate
that feeling as personal experience (*Erlebnisschema*) rather than
one derived from literature. The disjointed and alogical style of
Hausierer also creates a sense of fear within the reader: perhaps he

or she has not understood the content of the text. This latter fear drives the reader to create a sense of order out of narrative chaos. In this regard Handke has said, "Just as objects experienced in fear seem to have nothing to do with one another, in just such a way do sentences [in *Hausierer*] seem to have no relationship to each other."[15] A lack of specificity throughout the exposition or narrative portion of *Der Hausierer* creates "panic" or "fear" within the reader. Yet the reader's pleasure in reading the novel is found in its sense of play, in supplying those missing portions of the narrative that, in fact, the author has never provided.

Hausierer is a difficult text for any reader who tries to read it as a mystery about a specific murder. Like *Hornissen*, *Hausierer* is an open work of fiction in which the reader is invited to create his or her own understanding of the elements of the text. Characterized by indeterminacy, a prime aspect of postmodernist literature, *Hausierer* is all ambiguity, discontinuity, and randomness. If the novel never establishes a fixed identity for the peddler, or even offers any direct link between the peddler and the murderer, the reader nevertheless tries to reconstruct the details and the outline of a plot. *Hausierer* also challenges, even questions, the genre of the murder mystery within the wider context of literary merit. In its postmodernist manner, *Hausierer* affirms the writerly aspect of its text, raising it to the level of literary narrative discourse between the author and the reader. The underlying discourse of *Hausierer* revolves around the restoration of order from disorder. This novel is clearly a literary experiment by a writer who would try other literary methods in novels that followed *Hornissen* and *Hausierer*. In a 1976 interview Heinz Ludwig Arnold asked him whether he had "second thoughts" about anything he had recently written, and Handke replied, "Some things in my work are too smooth, those that are only formalistic from beginning to end, where nothing is contradictory, where a formal model is only that and nothing else. I have the feeling when I think of *Der Hausierer* that I wish I had written it another way" (Arnold, 18).

Die Angst des Tormanns beim Elfmeter

Peter Handke's third novel, *Die Angst des Tormanns beim Elfmeter* (1970; The Goalie's anxiety at the penalty kick), was internationally successful and extensively reviewed in both Germany and the United

States. The excellent 1972 English translation by Michael Roloff is the
first of many Roloff would make of Handke's works.[16] The first German edition numbered 25,000 copies. A film version co-written by
Handke and the director, his friend Wim Wenders, was released in
1972.[17] Their screenplay retains the basic outline of Handke's postmodernist text, but the film exchanges the novel's language-based
alienation for one grounded within the central character. The reasons for this transference lie in the basic esthetic differences
between directing a film and writing a novel. Wenders's chief problem was to find a filmic equivalent for those moments of language
crisis that punctuate the written text. The film was shown in New
York in 1972 as part of the New Directors/New Films series at the
Museum of Modern Art. This setting was an appropriate venue for
what is, for all intents and purposes, an "art" film, made for an audience willing to accept experimentation. Wenders's film was not available for general distribution in the United States until 1977, when it
rode the tide of German feature films directed by Fassbinder and
Herzog, whose work was no less accessible.

   "Handke," notes Jerome Klinkowitz, "writes detective novels in
a world influenced by Wittgenstein, Chomsky and other theoreticians
of language and perception of reality."[18] Strictly considered, however, *Angst* is not a genre murder mystery, though it generously
avails itself of that format, using motifs of pursuit, scattered clues,
and blind alleys to further its bare plot. The mystery of *Angst* is the
"mystery" that lies between perception and words; in Handke's
novel this conundrum is placed within the framework of a case study
(*Modellfall*) of a particular individual named Joseph Bloch.[19] Bloch,
in some respects a German Everyman, resembles Handke's Kaspar in
as much as he, like Kaspar, is the object of Handke's literary experiment about the effects of language alienation, but there the resemblance ends. Handke's range in *Angst* is broader, and his intentions
are quite different. The reader will remember that in *Kaspar* the title
figure is introduced by stages to the phenomenon of language-
speaking and then "abandoned" to the exigencies of language in
society. Bloch is exposed to the self-generating terror of words as
self-generating concepts, an idea that features Handke's
"fundamental distrust" of linguistic signs. Linstead has observed
other ways in which *Angst* is different from Handke's related studies
in language alienation (the *Sprechstücke*): "No longer do only words

and gestures have a normative, socializing function but all perception – particularly sound and vision – is seen to operate as if automatically, pre-formulated and internalized 'meanings' of experience dominate, so that individual acts of perception fit into a grid of expectation which prejudges their significance and places them within a system of coherence; the world becomes a mass of signs to be interpreted by the perceiver, the world mediates meanings" (1988, 83).

The first-time reader of *Angst* can thus anticipate that the novel is Handke's fictional exegesis of Wittgenstein's inquiry into language – that is, knowing what to say, how to know when one is saying it, and how to improve the "faulty" connection between one's inner self and the world's knowledge of it (Kauffmann 1972, 62). In his novel Handke places these fundamental questions within a phenomenological, semiotic context; *Angst* emerges as a conscious effort on the author's part to use semiotic principles in fiction. Among these principles is Handke's rejection of the notion that there is a fixed, bipartite relationship between a sign and a meaning, a word and a fixed interpretation (White, 234).

The plot of Handke's novel centers on the fate of Joseph Bloch, a retired goalie, now a mechanic. One Friday he thinks he has lost his job. That is the conclusion he draws from the fact that only the foreman looks up from his coffee when Bloch appears at the shack where other workers are standing about. Bloch then wanders through the streets of Vienna, reeling from the "fact" of his dismissal and gradually becoming disoriented by his perceptions of the outside world. The reader is introduced to a man whose mind might be disintegrating. He goes to the *Naschmarkt* and finds a sausage stand. He visits a movie theater, where the cashier takes his money in a "natural manner," thereby responding to Bloch's placing admission money before her. Bloch's response to these signs of normative behavior is one of surprise and amazement. He feels that he is reacting to a world of pretense and false simplicity, yet when he is mugged in the *Prater*, a victim of senseless violence and physical pain, he is much more interested in the sight of piled-up fruits and vegetables behind the stalls of the market. Their arrangements seem like a joke. Estranged from the linguistic and perceptive functions of the outer world, Bloch begins to feel not only that people do not mean what they say, but also that in their use of words there is a

code (a hieroglyph) he must crack, through which he will be able to
communicate. The reader senses that Bloch's attitude toward words
and signs is more important than the immediate reality of his environment. Unlike the sustained passive indifference of Camus's existentialist protagonist Meursault in *The Stranger* (1942), Bloch sub-
verts the behavior and language of others to form his private code of
linguistic discourse. Bloch's alienation, depicted at the beginning of
the text, comes from a source other than a sense of exclusion or
abandonment by society.

One night he goes home with the cashier from the box office of
the movie theater, for he is curious about her facility in coping with
words (signs) that come from the shared world of things that are not
only hers but also his. Bloch marvels that the girl uses a common system of signs and words that leaves her free to talk and move as she
chooses. The next morning in her apartment Bloch tires of the girl's
"chatter" and strangles her. He is clearly irritated at her having
anticipated not only his words but also his thought. (There are literary allusions to André Gide's *acte gratuit* in the apparently ruthless
and frivolous way that Bloch kills the girl.) In fact, however, the girl's
immediate words were simply ones asking him whether he planned
to go to work that day. Bloch misinterprets the intention of the question; he feels it is another instance of interference with his inner
world, an uncalled-for verbal penetration of his private thoughts.

Bloch subsequently flees by bus to a border village in the south
of Austria. He lodges near a tavern rented by a former girlfriend,
Hertha. In this idyllic village Bloch becomes trapped by language,
suffering the effects of an outsider's life and the isolation that began
in Vienna the previous Friday when he believed he had lost his job.
He wanders about the village visiting the frontier no-man's-land
between the end of the town and the border of the unnamed country, tracking down the life-style of his neighbors as well as himself.
He is, however, a murderer sought by the Viennese police. As yet he
is unaware that the police have linked the American coins he left
behind at the cashier's apartment with those found near the seat of
his riding companion, an older woman, in the bus south to the village. Bloch is as avid a reader of signs in the police reports concerning himself as he is a passionate, obsessive investigator of the
language system that continues to mediate between his perception
and the names of objects in the outside world. The narrative details

of Bloch's environment include remnants of a conversation between himself and a servant girl in the village inn and his interplay with customers in the local tavern. These prosaic happenings become the stuff of false impressions. In the early morning hours he confuses the sounds of a moving bus and the piling up of milk cans with those of a garbage truck.

Handke's exploitation in *Angst* of the connections between word signs and schizophrenia has led Schlueter to emphasize its status as a fictional study of mental abnormality or even of the psychopathology of language (1981, 85).[20] At several key points in the text Bloch believes that objects or people are forcing their presence upon him, demanding his attention. He believes, too, that these objects are issuing commands or directives. Fish-shaped cookies are sending out orders to act like a fish. A dishrag is expecting him to follow regulations. The cap of a bottle joins the "conspiracy" against him.

Here Bloch experiences mental and linguistic aberration in a twofold way. Signs for objects increasingly replace the objects themselves. This is a magical use of signs, rather than a normative one whereby a mentally stable person acknowledges their limited use. The magical use of signs, to which Bloch is very prone, is also abnormal in the sense that for Bloch objects become advertisements for themselves and are endowed with language and speaking facility (*Versprachlichung*). Toward the end of the novel Bloch moves from his initial position of language-perception skepticism to one of semiotic estrangement and dislocation.

Bloch's crisis with words precipitates two bouts with the "nausea" of language alienation (*Ekel*). In his room at the village inn, while his first experience of language nausea is incapacitating him, Bloch sees "everything with painful clarity." Handke notes, "Everything he saw was foreshortened. His nausea depressed him. He was pulled away forcefully from his surroundings and things like the clothes cupboard, a sink, a suitcase. He was forced to think of the word for each object" (*Angst*, 57).

Bloch's second bout with linguistic nausea occurs when he begins to see each object for itself, without translating it into words, as before, or comprehending it only in terms of words or word games. He enters a mental state in which everything seems natural. With verbalization absent, the very words themselves are rejected for a "primitive picture language: Bloch's version of mental hieroglyphics" (White, 248).

At the end of the novel Bloch goes to a soccer match and begins talking to a stranger. This is a conversation that Bloch clearly enjoys for its anonymity, and for a time he is mercifully free of having to transmit and receive messages. The stranger seems to be disturbed that there is no coach to instruct the players what to do from the sidelines of the game. Bloch, who is eager to talk and explain the working of the game to his companion, reveals much of himself and his special perspective on the world in the closing pages of the novel. To understand Bloch's words and the meaning behind the title of the text, Handke points out that throughout his adult life Bloch has felt a compulsion to interpret. This compulsion relates to his former status as a goalkeeper. The reader has already read the motto at the beginning of the novel: "The goalie watched as the ball rolled across the line." This first goalie has, however, lost the penalty kick. The image of failure depicted in this quote illuminates Bloch's adventures. He is a loser, or at the very least, a man who has lost rather than won.

Like the goalkeeper waiting between the posts for the penalty kick, Bloch is compelled to concentrate on signs and how they function in a triadic system – that is, the tenuous relationship between interpreter, sign, and referent. A goalkeeper feels (like Bloch) that he has no choice but to follow codes fixed by society. Bloch explains to his friend in the soccer stands as clearly as he can that during a penalty kick the spectator is well advised to take his eyes off the forward (the kicker) and watch the goalie instead. The spectator can then discern or even feel some of the goalie's tension and fear in interpreting and anticipating the moves and gestures of the kicker. Bloch thus emphasizes that the job for a spectator is to be able to read through the secret language or signs between the forward and the goalie. Will the kicker get his points by feigning a move into a false direction? Will the goalkeeper, Bloch asks, successfully anticipate the forward's tactics? At that moment a penalty kick is called on the soccer field, and Bloch, the former goalie, doubts that the goalie can stop the kick. For one thing, he says, the goalie running around without the ball, but expecting it, is "a strange sight" (*Angst*, 124). This is ridiculous activity, for as Bloch says when the kicker starts running, the goalkeeper may betray with his body, as he waits for the ball, which way he will throw himself. The kicker will then kick the other way.

But Bloch is proven wrong in this last and final reading of signs in the text: the penalty kicker shoots the ball into the goalie's hands. Interpreting the world of signs around him in his personal, solipsistic way, Bloch is still not free of the need to interpret and he cannot escape a system of mediation between himself and the outer world (Linstead 1987, 163). His fate – entrapment in the world of signs – is as threatening for him as it is for others in the novel, but it seems that his former profession of goalie only helps to intensify the problem, emphasizing the fear and anxiety with which he perceives his crisis. His dilemma includes portents of what might happen in the future. Bloch is not arrested by the police for the murder of the movie cashier in Vienna, though the reader can anticipate that this will occur. That Handke does not resolve this aspect of the plot, however, seems to indicate that solving the murder holds a low priority for him in the thematic strategy of the book. In *Angst* both Bloch and elusive, ambiguous language signs are objects of a hunt. Bloch has been living like the goalie waiting for the uncertain outcome of the penalty kick. If the soccer game, along with the close interaction of the kicker and the goalie, functions as a dominant metaphor for Bloch's predetermined confusion – between signs and himself as their interpreter – then this loss in the novel is a private, distorted one. Bloch's case is uniquely abnormal, involving the uncovering of a false language code at the cost of near mental and perceptive derangement. Transcendence, rather than confrontation, seems to be a solution to Bloch's dilemma of linguistic alienation, and Handke suggests this outcome when, at the end of the text, Bloch and the stranger witness the "success" of the goalie in stopping the penalty kick. The goalie wins because he has decided not to move or to use gestures or outward signs of any kind. There is nothing to interpret between the kicker and himself.

Angst is a contemporary European prose classic and an outstanding depiction of language-based alienation. Handke not only analyzes that alienation but restates the nature and substance of Bloch's dilemma in an original way for all readers.

Der kurze Brief zum langen Abschied

Der kurze Brief zum langen Abschied (1972; Short letter, long farewell) is Handke's fourth novel.[21] Its two-part title refers to its two main divisions. The "long farewell" alludes to themes of parting and separation, to the end of a relationship; it does not serve as a metaphor for death, as it does in Raymond Chandler's popular mystery, *The Long Good-bye* (1954). Like *Angst*, *Brief* features an alienated narrator-hero obsessed with signs and their meanings. Unnamed, he is estranged from events of his past life, reaching back to his birthplace in Austria, and has just arrived in America to start a new existence. The broad American setting of *Brief* shifts from the East Coast to the Pacific Northwest, and American readers can view their country and its culture through the distanced perspective of a European who resembles Handke. Though Handke has denied any direct link between his narrator and himself, the book's episodes and setting correspond with the time during which Handke made a lecture tour of the United States.

In an interview with Helmuth Karasek in 1972, Handke noted that "the novel is about a journey, but not a report of that journey. One might say that it is a departure journey, a leave-taking from a definite, daily way of living."[22] The narrator travels, in fact, from Providence to New York and then to Philadelphia, picking up the trail of his vindictive wife, Judith, who has followed him to America and is out to kill him. She communicates with him through short letters (hence the title of the novel) and possessions she leaves behind. The narrator resumes a former liaison with Claire, an American teacher of German, and this part of the book offers deeper insight into the tangled state of his emotional and personal affairs. Claire and her child, Benedictine, function as interpreters of American culture and history for Handke's narrator. All three go to St. Louis, a prototypical midwestern American city. This trip evolves, especially through stylistic devices such as conversation and dialogue, into an allegorical and symbolic reading of the American cultural landscape: Claire points out subtle and differing aspects of America to the Austrian visitor, reflected through her image-oriented understanding of history. In St. Louis, a city settled by German immigrants, the pair attend a performance of Schiller's drama *Don Carlos*, given by a troupe of German actors. Claire explains why the play can fail before an American audience, which might not relate to a European's expectation that history is a record of achievements by the "role players" – that is, the leading historical figures. Americans prefer to view the "action" or "movement" behind historical events. The didactic, instructive aspects of *Brief* resemble the structure of a bildungsroman, a Germanic novel of education, which involves the protagonist and the reader in a learning process that conveys ideas within the framework of an integrating concept of character development (Karasek, 88). The goal of the traditional German bildungsroman has always been to integrate its protagonist into mainstream society, and at the end of *Brief* Handke's narrator is seemingly directed toward this objective.

Yet other aspects of *Brief* are important – namely, its tendency to move into the genre of the adventure tale (Scharang, 85). The book includes a confrontation between the narrator and his wife in an Oregon lumber town, where she takes out a gun and threatens to kill him. Handke never tells the reader directly why Judith fails to murder her husband, nor does the author reveal how she is so easily disarmed. This episode has a texture of unreality, and the narrator cannot recall the exact details. The novel concludes with the couple's reconciling visit to the home of the iconographic American film director John Ford, from whom they learn how to reorder and reformulate their disrupted lives. They are taught the American way of communal thinking (the content of group consensus) as a means for resolving conflict. Ford says that Americans (in contrast to Europeans), for example, use "we" instead of "I" when referring to their private business. Ford sees Europeans as people dominated by their subjective selves.

The couple agree in the end to part peacefully, partially because of Ford's mediation and partially because of the narrator's newly acquired and deeply honed sensitivity to the causes of human dissension. He applies to himself the lessons he has learned in America. His decision to leave America is a gift to his wife: he is allowing her the freedom to follow her own path of self-evolution. This solution, Handke implies, was inconceivable at the beginning of the narrator's journey and could only have been reached in the neutral context and with the distancing perspective afforded the two Europeans by their American cultural experience.

The narrator's trip to America begins ostensibly as a voyage of self-discovery and education. He wants a new and different identity, but fear is also a key reason for his quest for liberation from his past. He says that he seems to have been born for fear and horror (*Brief*, 9). When he arrives at his hotel in Providence and the clerk gives him a letter from Judith, he is overcome by a childhood dream (a memory) of death by American bomber planes. This is an early sign that his perception of things and people in America is still troubled by lingering remnants of the past. He realizes, too, that geographical distance, even the vast distance between Europe and America, has failed to resolve the quiddity of memory. For example, the note from Judith and fears about her death prompt the memory of climbing a rocky hill, as a young boy, to look for his mother and learning she had jumped over to commit suicide. Bruno Hillebrand notes that the narrator, though susceptible to fear and horror, is nevertheless not a fatalist, for he believes that he can change his life positively, reflecting growth and development.[23] The narrator's will to change, says Hillebrand, is an important element in this process: it brought him to America and makes him a figure who stands out in the reader's mind, in contrast to the protagonist of *Angst*, who runs away from city life in Vienna to the obscurity of an Austrian village. The narrator in *Brief* expects much from his new country and is receptive to continually new impressions: the neutrality of the American landscape; conversation with Claire about Americans; the mythology of American history. Even his opportunity to contrast minor cultural details between Austria and America becomes important, and the strangeness of America is the perfect foil to the fledgling narrator for achieving that distance and objectivity needed to contrast elements of his life in America to his Austrian past. The reader must realize that Handke's narrator needs to shed a superabundance of self-centered egoism and introspection. As Handke has noted, in America one is "unburdened" and "depersonalized" and becomes a type, not an individual (Scharang, 87).

A leading leitmotiv in *Brief* is Handke's continual references to works of fiction and their central characters.[24] These references are not only autobiographical in the sense that Handke has often reflected on the positive ability of fiction to change or influence life; they function also to reflect, negate, or clarify the subjective aspirations of the narrator. In *Brief* there are two quotations from Karl Philip Moritz's psychological novel *Anton Reiser*, whose character undertakes a journey of education similar to that of Handke's narrator, yet with negative results. Two other books mentioned in *Brief* serve, however, as inspirational models for the narrator's reflections in his new American environment: F. Scott Fitzgerald's *The Great Gatsby* and Gottfried Keller's *Green Henry*. The first novel is notable for its American image of the unhappy, romantic male, contemplating his beloved from a mansion across the bay from her; the second book, a nineteenth-century Swiss bildungsroman, has a European setting and features the odyssey of a young man who leaves home, goes to a big city to study, and returns home a professional failure as an artist but a wiser human being. Keller's novel stresses the higher necessity of communal over individual values.

Reading *Green Henry* is, in *Brief*, a catalyst for the narrator's own reflections on nature; he is astonished to learn that when Henry moved to the country he experienced freedom in nature and looked at it with curious pleasure. In his American setting the narrator realizes that as a youth in the country he had hated nature rather than adored it. Nature was oppressive (*bedrückt*), not life-giving. He had been forced to work in nature. Handke's point is manifold – namely, that the narrator's valuable insight occurs within the context of American culture, and that he is learning to place the "horror" of his Austrian childhood memories behind him. The narrator's sensitivity to Gatsby's fate in Fitzgerald's novel marks a similar instance of inner growth. Gatsby, a man who bought a home on a particular bay solely for the purpose of seeing the lights in a house inhabited by a woman whom he could never love, incites the narrator's sympathy for Judith. He wonders whether the feelings engendered through reading *Gatsby* – happiness, generosity, and goodwill – can be transferred to his new setting and environment (*Brief*, 18).

These reflections, derived from the narrator's readings of Fitzgerald, denote incipient growth and compassion for the individuality of others and signal that he at least is willing to consider life on another level of experience. In another incident that corroborates this new sensitivity, the newly arrived visitor to America enters a bar in Providence and has a brief encounter with a pair of dice players who invite him to join their game. He throws his dice in a way that impels him to see his desired number moving through another dimension of time: "All the dice but one came to rest and it continued to roll between the glasses. The number I needed flashed up and vanished, and another number was on top. And yet I felt that number had really come up – not now but AT SOME OTHER TIME. This other time was not in the future or in the past, it was essentially a time OTHER than the time in which I lived or thought" (*Brief*, 25). For the narrator, this experience portends possibility and hope. It is a personal vision of the probability of change, yet it is too brief to be permanent and enduring.

A similar incident, with a related aftermath portending the possibility of change in the character's consciousness and leading him onto another level of sensibility, occurs in Handke's later novel *Die Stunde der wahren Empfindung* and the various novels that make up the *Langsame Heimkehr* tetralogy. In *Brief* "another time" (*eine andere Zeit*) is significant because it connotes the sense of possibility in the narrator's quest for change, especially the probability that his wish for personal renewal may come true. In America the narrator becomes attuned to the symbolic meaning of signs, and in this sense the number on the rolling die becomes such a sign. For the reader, the meaning of the episode is significant on at least two levels of interpretation: the mystical and the utopian. The narrator intuitively perceives what has taken place in the wider context of his role as a free agent in control of his own destiny, and at this point "another time" is "expectancy." The narrator is impelled to continue his American journey.[25]

Moving south from Providence to New York and then to Philadelphia, the narrator joins his friend Claire on a motor trip to St. Louis. Claire is the "other woman" in the novel but does not endure as a chief player in the narrator's romantic and sexual life. As Handke has pointed out, Claire is intended to be "the point from which the hero tries to learn something about America and through whom he hopes to know America" (Scharang, 85). In the novel Claire is the "model educator" to the "apprentice traveler" within the framework of the mandatory discussion that is often a standard feature of the bildungsroman. As Handke's Austrian narrator begins to perceive Claire as the ideal American, she becomes the vehicle through which America and American culture survive in the novel, not as "an object of criticism, but rather the instrument of awakening for the protagonist" (Schlueter 1981, 98).

Claire and her child become important factors in Handke's portrayal of life in America, for their daily lives are determined by American signs and their literal meanings. Their American consciousness has absorbed the systematized mythology of American everyday life and its encounter with the American historical past: the "honesty" of George Washington; the "perilous" landing of the pilgrims at Plymouth Rock; the legend of Sir Walter Raleigh smoking Virginia tobacco. Benedictine adheres to a system of American signs that is uniquely her own. Claire explains this system to the narrator during a cross-country trip, and in listening to Claire Handke's protagonist has a lesson in the American way of living with "signs" or words as they define human illusion and truth. American signs, says Claire, survive in the American psyche as guideposts to security and permanence in the apparent neutrality of American culture. She also explains how this behavioral complex relates to her continuous nurturing of Benedictine. Among the "mistakes" she made in nurturing her child was to use many names rather than only one. Using many names, says Claire, confused her daughter, as Benedictine no longer had a unique, special name for herself. The foregoing story impresses the narrator as a parable of child-rearing in America (*Brief*, 85).

Benedictine's fear, Claire explains, is associated with the sense of a loss of stability that comes about through the use of "many" words. The narrator, who listens to Claire attentively, is relieved to find that he has stopped feeling the fear in his memory of the past – that is, his guilt over an unhappy childhood that he realizes relates to that of Benedictine. He admits to Claire that, in his own case, "states of fear coming from his youthful reading of signs were turned into . . . ways of knowledge. . . . If I had moments of hope in those days, I've forgotten them" (*Brief*, 76). The narrator, even in America, is not free of the need to talk, draw comparisons, and thus learn about his past life. Active, not passive, memory plays an important role in the narrator's recall of the past: "The thought that something else lies somewhere else, and that I can't be there immediately, drives me crazy, just as it did as a child. . . . I'm talking about all of this, so that I might feel less isolated than before" (*Brief*, 96-97). In response, Claire warns her friend against the euphoria of premature "false" detachment and drifting away from everyday reality in the manner of Green Henry, who, in his "wisdom," made "no attempt to decipher anything, one event would simply follow from another" (*Brief*, 97). This observation seems to end the possibility of Green Henry's education serving as a viable role model for the narrator and implies that Claire has had the last word. The reader anticipates a deeper resolution of the narrator's existing quest for an answer to the problems of his inner life.

When the narrator and Claire arrive in St. Louis, he has a chance to observe the workings of an intimate relationship analogous to his with Judith. The St. Louis "lovers," as Claire freely calls them, are her friends, but like his friendship with Claire, their relationship serves as an object of observation and curiosity for the narrator. Using comparison and contrast as devices of understanding, the narrator is anxious to study the lovers' mode of life and to examine the effects of a suffocating relationship in which their affection for each other is so strong that it borders on irritation. The lovers cling to, embrace, and caress one another in a ritualistic code of responses. The man, who is a painter, will not sketch anything that has never existed in historical reality; he paints only true historical moments in historical landscapes. Here the narrator makes a telling observation on the depiction of history in American painting: "I realized that all the pictures I had seen so far in America, those in Providence and other hotels, had never been fantasies; they were all reproductions from American history" (*Brief*, 119). The painter's wife explains that this oddity is a consequence of the general American belief that landscapes derive their meaning from their history and as backdrops for the deeds of the men who conquered America. America, the narrator learns from this couple, is a country with signs whose meanings often allude to historical events and issues.

In his approach to American culture and history (and painting), Handke laudably avoids projecting his private symbolism of American life on the reader and chooses rather to explain how American symbols control his plot, especially the ongoing "education" of the narrator himself (Barry 1987, 109). He is sympathetic to the eccentricities of American culture, past and present, and to the Americanized "theatrical revelation of history," as the St. Louis lovers demonstrate. Yet his narrator, a European visitor to the New World, shares Handke's lingering belief in the vital forces of the American dream. Acceptance rather than rejection enters the narrator's consciousness in key moments of positive reflection during the end of his stay in St. Louis: "At that time, I felt a longer, more sustained sense of being. . . . I felt content with myself. I scarcely moved, no longer thought only about myself . . . everything happened by itself, without tension, as the result of a natural flow of life" (*Brief*, 122).

The narrator has learned a lot on his trip with Claire, the most profound lessons being his new awareness that if he has not become another person, he has found a way into his inner self. As Barry has noted, "The juxtaposition of America's past and present, fiction and fact . . . cause the protagonist to reflect upon reality and his own life in a more positive sense, that is, certain fictions . . . present alternative visions of other possible realities from which the individual can learn" (1987, 110).

Especially liberating for the protagonist is his therapeutic dialogue with Claire about the roots of his deadening relationship with Judith and the subsequent metamorphosis of their intimacy into enmity and reification. They were both defenseless against their nerves. They no longer could think about anything except themselves. He admits to Claire that he is prepared to give up on Judith, despite her threat of murdering him. Judith, always in the habit of striking poses, becomes for the narrator the image of a suffering woman, hence a forgivable one.

The alternative vision of "another time," experienced earlier in the novel, is reevaluated by the narrator under a different set of conditions – namely, after making love to Claire. The narrator's love for Claire (and her contiguous American world) symbolizes his return to normal social intimacy with a woman. The "paradise" forecast in the earlier vision of "another time," on the other hand, is perceived as an empty and barren place, "one without life or love," an illusion that can be confused with the truth and reality (*Brief*, 101). The narrator loses his desire to shed his identity. He confronts his fears, his avoidance of other people. He accepts his limitations as normal human limitations.

The novel's advocacy of signs and words derived from the grammar of American film provides another life-saving vision for the protagonist. Handke's book points out that American feature films play an important part in the narrator's understanding and decoding of American history, and that these films, especially those directed by John Ford, explicate "a still valid system of myth that incorporates particular objects and actions within a functional system of signification" (Klinkowitz and Knowlton, 50). Like Handke, the narrator is an admirer of John Ford, whose film *Young Mr. Lincoln* (1939) he attends in St. Louis. The film's historic American theme and setting are, for the narrator, inspired acts of self-identity and the common-weal. While viewing the film he dreams of his future, and the actors on the screen forecast happy and contented people, his future friends. American film is an augury, a sign, of his new life.

When the narrator and his wife meet John Ford in Hollywood, they have the nightmare of the aborted shooting in Oregon behind them. Their extended conversation with Ford includes much of what the narrator had absorbed previously from Claire and his St. Louis experience, and if Ford's ideas are not exactly new, they are never-theless backed up by the director's creative reflections on the unique essence of the American cultural experience, of which Ford under-stands himself to be an authentic interpreter. The narrator notes Ford's refusal to judge people, preferring only to tell what they have done. No American, Ford says, thinks anyone else in America is spe-cial, and the saving grace of the American psyche, as opposed to the European one, is its lack of extreme subjectivity. The narrator has no choice, it seems, but to accept the world and himself as they are at this point in time. Overcoming his fear of existence is something that only an American perspective could have given him. America affords the means of dealing with the fact that to be alive is to be fearful, and it gives him the wonderful freedom to part from Judith in a generous and tolerant way. Judith, however, has not escaped the impact of self-evaluation as a result of her impetuous American journey. She will leave the country, too, with changed perspectives on herself and the world about her.

The story of the narrator and Judith in America is destined to lose its original contours and the factual basis of its fundamental antagonism over a period of time. Fact and realism in the anonymity of American cultural experience, the novel states, will move onto a level of parareality, resting finally in a place where forgiveness re-places fear and enmity.[26] In this sense *Brief* is a positive work and ends with the possibility of resolution of what was originally a mortal conflict.

Chapter Four

Mature Fiction

A Memoir, 1972

Handke's *Wunschloses Unglück* (A Sorrow beyond dreams) appeared in 1972 and is subtitled "A Story," though it is a short biography in that it highlights episodes from the tragic life of Handke's mother, who committed suicide at the age of 51, in her native village of Altenmarkt.[1] Handke decided to put his memories of her unfortunate life into words, both to relieve the depth of his grief and to assuage the extremity of his "speechlessness" at her death. Biography is broadly defined as a written account of a person's life, a life history that should be preserved. The impetus for the writing of biography might arise from a commemorative instinct or even a didactic and moralistic intention, recalling the high social status of the deceased. Twentieth-century biography, however, can choose any figure as its subject, upon which it will typically focus with intense scrutiny. A modern writer of biography prefers to be objective in assessing the subject's ethical and moral qualities. *Unglück*, a contemporary biography, is a document sui generis, an original example of its genre.[2] Its subject, Peter Handke's mother, was neither high-born nor socially distinguished. The short span of her life, and its tragic outcome, become a probing matter for Handke to resolve and explicate.

But *Unglück* is also a wider account of young Handke's family life, and it is here that the reader can enter the book. The reader first learns about the character of Handke's German stepfather, who married his mother when she was pregnant with him. Maria Handke was an Austrian war bride who loved and married under the national euphoria of the Austrian Anschluss in 1938. In the text Handke rarely mentions his other siblings, but he does refer to his several years of moving about between Germany and Austria with his itinerant, root-

less mother. Critics, citing the personal tone of the book, have valued it for the biographical details gleaned from its narrative (Demetz,
226). Yet one discovers that *Unglück* is an endeavor to transcend the
traditional limitations of biographical structure. Handke is interested
as a writer in deconstructing traditional biographical methodology,
and he does this through a postmodernist technique that is new,
unique, and analytical to a high degree. In this book Handke separates the narrative text relating to his mother's life from commentary
on his methodology; those portions describing theory and method
are usually set off by parentheses and qualifying statements. In these
sections the author reveals *how* he wrote his book.

That one should learn how the book was written, however, is no
great surprise, since the viability of literary methodology has been a
perennial concern of Handke, informing efforts like his language
pieces and several full-length plays, such as *Kaspar* and
Bodensee – two works distinguished by originality of dramatic
method. Both *Hornissen* and *Hausierer* deconstruct fiction and the
very act of novel writing. Deconstruction for Handke is no mere
esthetic exercise; it is always allied to undermining the natural and
"erroneous" connections between language and reality. In his 1967
"Bewohner" essay, Handke points out the fallacy of assuming that
there is a fixed literary method for any one literary genre (20). He
further states that traditional models of literary genres have outlived
their usefulness. Their frequent use has trivialized literature and
made the artist's concept of reality questionable. The reality of a literary text, Handke claims, can only be the reality of the artist-writer
functioning in his role as the creator of a new text. It follows that
Handke should make the claim that he tries to find a new literary
method for every book, whether it be a play, a novel, or a biography.
This necessary renewal of literary methodology moves Handke to
question the nature of art and reality. In *Unglück* this reality lies
within the profundity of the grief he suffers over the suicide of his
mother. The text reveals the means by which this grief is made real,
and the reader is carried through the dualistic stages of the book's
narrative and its artistic process.

If the primacy of literary method was an issue in Handke's early
years as a writer, and if method was linked by Handke to the writer's
reality (Handke would assert, the only reality), then the opening
pages of *Unglück* demonstrate the vitality of this emphasis outside

the realm of theater and fiction. Here Handke states clearly that writing about his mother's suicide is his own business, since he clearly knew more about her and the circumstances leading to her death than any interviewer who might rely on "outside" help of a religious, psychological, or sociological kind to unravel this case of an "interesting suicide." Writing, says Handke, is for him a means of personal revitalization ("whenever I have something to do"). Lastly, writing this book will give him the chance to show a *voluntary death* (*Freitod*) as an *exemplary* one (*Unglück*, 10).

This passage at the book's opening reveals the author's deep interest in setting down the record; he has the right, he feels, more than any stranger, to speak for his mother's life and suicide. And he is no outsider, no interviewer whose expertise might exclude "subjectivity," an aspect of the book that Handke feels is needed for a balanced appraisal of the tragedy. Yet as an artist Handke makes the astonishing claim that "having something to do" – this can only mean the writing of the biography – is part of his project. Handke has said elsewhere that literature has been his great teacher of life, so this book, in a special sense, is concerned with the *making* of a text as a life-informing device (literature as revitalization). Lastly, in the above passage the reader is drawn toward the didactic parallel between "voluntary" and "exemplary," the idea that a voluntary act of suicide was an exemplary act. The reader is left wondering, however, whether Handke's real goal in the book is only to demonstrate that his mother was a victim of the exemplary, structured life forced upon her by the mores of her Austrian village. In a commentary on this passage, Linstead notes, "From birth her biography is seen [by Handke] to have been determined according to what women can and cannot do, by the male-dominated society in which she lived. The portrayal of her life, the public form it takes, must not then be such that it again, in its turn, only fits that life into an established representation of it. The problem [for Handke] is how to fit her biography into public, yet individual sentences" (1987, 164-65).

Handke is aware, however, of two dangers: "only telling what happened or only allowing that person to disappear in poetic sentences" (*Unglück*, 42). Yet he feels that he must start with society's "formulations" (clichés) of a woman's life within her time so that he can show, by contrast, how they are related to the particulars of his mother's life. The agreements and contradictions between his mother's public and private lives can thus emerge and become an integral part of Handke's deconstructive biographical method and concept of balance, functioning between the abstraction of social formulation and the realism of an actual life.

There are three main segments of Handke's narrative-biographical text.[3] The first begins with his mother's birth "more than fifty years ago" in Altenmarkt and ends in 1948. The second segment relates those events from 1948 through the suicide itself in Altenmarkt in 1971; the third describes the burial ceremony and the author's initial period of mourning. Handke wrote *Unglück* from January to February 1972. In the initial segment Handke begins with a description of his mother's parents and her birth. Her ancestors and her parents sired a stable of manual laborers and farmers in Carinthia, where living conditions in the 1920s were identical to those of 1848, a pivotal year in the struggle of European liberalism against conservative German and Austrian politics. Handke's grandfather was a carpenter and inherited a farm that he fought to keep. Through war and inflation he would lose his savings, money that he had hoped to pass on to his sons, for only a man's sons were considered a serious "family investment." The birth of a girl was a nonevent.

Maria Handke was next to the last of five children, and she was reared to spend her life within the traditional parameters of home, church, and family, paying tribute to her brothers' hegemony within the family circle of siblings and to the prevailing wisdom of the village community. Handke states that a girl's future was a joke in the hands of a fortune-teller, but it was still expected to follow the steps of "a child's game based on the stages of womanhood – namely, 'Tired/Exhausted/Sick/Dying/Dead'" (*Unglück*, 17). At this point of the text Handke tries to reconstruct key events in his young mother's life. This is a technique that includes remembered stories of her life (told by her to him) along with his own commentary upon them. He subjects his mother's dreams to social and political analysis. Proper language, restrained gestures, and ethical behavior were three outstanding features of society's rules for young unmarried women.

Helmut Scheffel points out the thematic analogy between the Handke character Kaspar and Maria Handke that can be found in the learning process to which both were subjected.[4] If Kaspar learns to speak only to lose his individuality through language, he remains an abstract example of Handke's thesis in the guise of a model figure. But Handke's mother is far from abstract; she is a concrete instance of a woman drawn from the background of early twentieth-century Austrian village life.

Maria Handke left home between 15 and 16 to work as a cook in a hotel. She was not missed by her parents, and her absence was tolerated as the eccentric gesture of a young girl. The family knew instinctively that she would go "nowhere" and eventually return home. Her foray into city life and urban fashions (short skirts), along with her hidden fear of sex (appropriate behavior for an Austrian country girl), were interrupted by the Anschluss on 10 April 1938. Handke interpolates the dreams of his mother about the future she saw for herself in the new political order. There would be a progressive role for women in the one state. A strange and incomprehensible world acquired order and meaning for the young woman. For Maria Handke, Nazi Austrian politics meant feminine pride and being alive with a rising level of consciousness. Handke notes that World War II was not the equivalent of the childhood horror that would determine her future life, as it did his own. For her the war was the experience of a fantastic world (*Unglück*, 25). Though his mother became an unwitting victim of Nazi political sloganeering and the totalitarian government that engendered it, she fell in love with a German paymaster of the Wehrmacht, a married man with whom she conceived her son Peter. This affair was the only romance of her life. Certain of its episodes are recalled in the text: reading books together, receiving a gift of perfume, running down the mountain pastures under "embarrassing" circumstances. These were simple, primitive pleasures, normally forgotten in the passing of time, yet they stayed with Handke's mother even after she made the wrong decision – out of a sense of social duty – to marry Bruno Handke, a German army sergeant who courted her with the intent of marrying her, despite the stigma of taking on another man's child.

Handke dwells here on the debilitative effects of social and ethical conformity, especially the shame of bearing a child without a father. This was a commitment, Handke insists, made by his mother under dishonest conditions. Here the book shows the reader that Maria Handke's life was already moving toward its predictable outcome of suicide; its tragedy would come from her gradual depersonification, the confluence of inner and external pressures urging her to "be sensible," to "listen to reason." She desired to survive the shame of not having a husband. She had an obligation to give her child a father. In her new role as the wife of an German army sergeant, living in East Berlin, she learned to budget objects and people, as she would later learn to save money, repressing her emotions and feelings in the process and losing the distinction, as Handke notes, between reason and spontaneity. She was moving away from the mental and spiritual complex of individuality toward the narrowly channeled definition of a "**type**."[5] (The boldface print is Handke's own stylistic device denoting his deconstruction of words.) In moving from a young female type to that of a married woman, Maria hoped to escape the social censure that was ready to castigate deviancy and eccentricity. She was thus freed from her dubious history by seeing herself through the eyes of an erotic stranger (*Unglück*, 38). The stranger was, Handke suggests, society and its judgmental attitudes. Typology, an insidious but pragmatic way to define the sexes and establish social control between them, became a general guide to living in both the city and the village, a *vade mecum* that insulated the bearer of a social tag (a type) from whatever might fall accidentally into his or her sphere of influence. If there was a business type and an artistic type, there was also an ideal expressed in a feminine type. Handke calls this social stratification a strategy for bourgeois survival, but it was only a subterfuge for poverty and suffering in Maria's Berlin life. The fact was that she was a dependent woman living on welfare money who begged strangers to give her husband a chance to keep his job.

When she returned with her husband and two children (Peter and a daughter born in Berlin) to Austria in the summer of 1948, Maria Handke was determined to shed the growing conflict between herself and the "eternal stringency" that prevented her from imagining another kind of life. She resumed her native Austrian dialect and was content to be known as the villager who had once lived abroad (Germany). These several instances of individuality within the traditional complex of village life, however, were minor examples of many efforts to extricate herself from a way of living that continued to estrange her through religious practices and proper social behavior. Schlueter (1981, 127) and Miles (377), in their separate critical studies of *Unglück*, both point out that Handke uses the language of postmodernist realism to turn his mother into a sociological case study of defamiliarization. This linguistic realism is actually a decon-structive technique that purposely deviates from what is commonly understood as a realistic style, such as the broad, digressive kind of realism favored by Goethe in the early nineteenth century or even the ironic realism of Thomas Mann in a family-history novel like *Buddenbrooks* (1925). Handke's realism in *Unglück* is metonymic in nature – that is, it dwells on an essential realistic detail and lets that detail stand for the whole. As in Kafka's novels, the stress on periph-eral details in Handke's text seems to overwhelm the reader's con-cept of a conventional reality, especially one to which he or she might refer. Miles comments on characteristics of Handke's realism in *Unglück* and how it works to provide his unique portrait of truth and valid experience: "This model, growing out of 19th century realism, defines itself by its defamiliarization, deconstruction and dis-tortion of all inherited models of what was once presumed to be 'reality.' A central method in this estrangement or alienation from what had become routine is the close-up" (375).

A key passage in the second segment of *Unglück* can be used to demonstrate the metonymic method firsthand. Handke had the adjectives in this passage specifically set in boldface type: "a **threat-ening** thimble, a **dumb** darning egg, a **shaky** flat iron" (*Unglück*, 60). Other adjectives – *cozy, funny,* and *dangerous* – also charac-terize these household and kitchen items. Realism in this passage is far from informative in the traditional sense of a writer telling the reader about the actual contents of the kitchen or other rooms of a house. The excerpt is instead a parody working on several levels of surprise, especially on the levels of advertising (the capital letters) and cinematic technique (the focused words). As Miles has noted, "The idyllic realism of the whole passage is an illusion paralleled by the 19th century adjectives" (376). Maria Handke is shown to be living in a world of illusory language and words not of her own making. Her suicide is thus reflected in the "death" of a realism that utterly fails to convey the stuff of realism. The highlighted adjectives advertise linguistic and human defamiliarization. Even Maria Handke's domestic reality became a mass reality that contributed to her alienation.

Unglück is not only an examination of the linguistic and social reasons underlying the suicide of Handke's mother but also the story of Handke as an observer and recorder of that event. What he

reports about the last years of her life in her native village is revealing, especially the record of her depression and medical treatment,
for it was difficult to get a diagnosis of her illness. At the end of her
life she began to read books, especially to compare the outcome of a
fictional life with her own. She often claimed that she was "not like
that" (*Unglück*, 63). Yet, as Handke points out, she scarcely read literature as a catalyst for personal change. Her reading of literature
was never what it became for Handke, a teacher and even a liberator
from moral and ethical strictures. Literature was always showing her
that it was too late to start again. She had internalized inner and
social pressures to such a degree that, in a key scene that Handke
recounts (and imagines), she begs him, lying on her bed, to plead
her "case" in writing, as Kafka had done for the character of the
stoker in his 1927 novel *Amerika* (in which Karl Rossmann tries to
intercede for that humiliated man, who is being tried and judged in
the docked ship at its harbor in New York).

Handke's mother's suffering is real and literature-related, and
her request becomes for Handke an artist's reason to write the book.
This is a promise, however, that he decides to keep only later, when
he is on a plane returning to Austria for his mother's funeral and
realizes that her suicide was actually a refusal to compromise a
dream of another, better life. He is proud that she committed suicide. Handke decides finally that his mother opted for a voluntary
death while living in a knowing way under the lie of an exemplary
existence. Yet as the writer of a text for which he had hoped earlier
to find a new literary method, an artistic compromise between biography and the particulars of a singular life, Handke is not entirely
satisfied. His book begins to disintegrate in its last pages. He relates
idiosyncratic episodes of dubious relevancy: his mother wiping out
the children's ears and nostrils with her saliva, cutting slices of bread
into warm milk, hoarding an eggnog bottle in the sideboard. Handke
is careful to keep the details of his story from overwhelming his
reader. He also makes an ambiguous promise to the reader to be
more exact in the future. The reader is not sure whether grief has
taken over or Handke's writing has collapsed. The reader also senses
that Handke wishes to stress the analogy between his failure to do
justice to the details of his mother's life and the writing of the book
itself. In the book's open ending, Handke admits that writing has not
helped him to overcome his sorrow, that narration in his case has

degenerated into an "act" of memory, holding "nothing in reserve for future use. . . . From enjoyment of horror it produces enjoyment of memory" (*Unglück*, 67). Frank Kermode sums up the book well: "The 'idiocy' of his mother's life becomes his own idiocy, and the story becomes an account of his own horror, characterized as *horror vacui*, the source of the very language he uses, in all its fallibility and corruption, is now frozen" (23).

Two Postmodernist Novels, 1975-1976

Die Stunde der wahren Empfindung

Handke's short novel *Die Stunde der wahren Empfindung* (1975; A Moment of true feeling) was written in Paris, during the summer and autumn of 1974.[6] *Stunde* relates thematically to his two previous novels, *Angst* and *Brief*, stressing similar ideas of alienation and disorientation. In *Stunde* there are allusions to Kierkegaard's sense of religious alienation, Sartre's existential nausea and the metaphorical transformation of Gregor Samsa, the central character of Kafka's novella *The Metamorphosis* (1915). These broad analogies to major writers in the European existentialist tradition are important because in each of these three novels Handke defines a different aspect of alienated experience, which he proposes to resolve in a separate way for each text. *Angst* is Handke's quintessential novel of alienation through language, of the dichotomy between language signs and reality in the everyday world of language communication. Joseph Bloch learns to accept the inherent "madness" between words and meanings as a necessity for basic communication. The American journey of Handke's Austrian narrator in *Brief* not only defines but also resolves the alienated experience of his odyssey within the context of American culture. *Brief* also introduces Handke's notion of release from alienation through "another time," the intense vision of an epiphany that is best understood as a phase of Handke's creative vision of a conflict-free, unalienated existence. This vision in *Brief* occurs at an unexpected moment in time.

In *Brief* it is the film director John Ford, known for his westerns, who functions as Handke's explicator of a conflict-free existence. Ford incorporates a "working myth" that is reflected in the history of the United States and its national culture. The nation's history, Ford suggests to Handke's narrator and his estranged wife, is rife with "messages" conducive to resolving the effects of alienation. Ford's conversation with the pair, coming as it does at the end of *Brief*, thus offers a "fantastic," postmodernist response to a major theme of the novel.

The plot of *Stunde*, in contrast with those of *Angst* and *Brief*, is simple and accessible. Gregor Keuschnig, a married Austrian press attaché working as a diplomat at his country's embassy in Paris, follows a prototypical life for a European diplomat. His daily routine includes arriving early at his office to read French newspapers for references to Austrian politics, culture, and society. He is invited to press conferences at the Elysée Palace. A major source of Gregor's alienation in the novel is his profession as a reader and writer, a "proofreader" who corrects the reports of the French press about Austrian life. The artificiality of language, especially the false imagery of language in the world of journalism, throws Gregor off balance. For him, the discovery that the rituals of everyday life can undermine language leads to stasis, anger, and disorientation. He begins to suffer from the sociolinguistic effects of the system under which he labors. Gregor has a mistress, Beatrice, who is almost indifferent to his lovemaking, yet he lives under the illusion that he controls this relationship, a secret part of his life. Though he loves his child, Agnes, Gregor is making plans to leave his wife, Stefanie. One night, however, Gregor's life is changed forever when he has a dream in which he murders an old woman. This dream is the fictional device in Handke's text by which Gregor is dropped past a demarcation line and into another level of reality from which he can never fully return. Here a thematic resemblance to Gregor Samsa in Kafka's *Metamorphosis* is evident. *Stunde* is subsequently concerned with the texture and meaning of this alienated experience, one that Gregor suffers alone in the twilight world of Handke's novel. Gregor is Handke's exclusive vehicle for the depiction of this change, and for most of the novel's duration Gregor lives a dualistic existence, one that shifts between his role as a model Austrian diplomat and that of an imposter, a rebel in a conventional social system.

One can assume that Gregor, as a career diplomat, is a likely candidate for any kind of change for its own sake. Years of structured living have led him to suppress his feelings and emotions. The novel's epigraph, however, from the writings of Max Horkheimer, the

German political philosopher, gives the reader a hint of Handke's future intentions regarding Gregor's fate: "Violence and inanity – are they not ultimately one and the same thing?" Handke thus intends us to understand that the murder in Gregor's dream and his dreamt role as a murderer are visually and internally expressed equivalents of social violence, the twofold consequence of Gregor's inane, alienated life. The dream is, of course, powerful enough to initiate real change in Gregor's life and jar him out of his protective routine. This change makes him fear the shame of social ostracism, so he is forced to simulate conventional activity: eating with others and answering harmless, friendly questions about himself. Because of the murder he is ashamed before his parents. The old woman lies in a coffin. A murderer in the family! He is oppressed by the idea that he has turned into someone else but has to continue living with his former self (*Stunde*, 8).

How Gregor manages to function between the two worlds becomes for the reader a central focus for explicating the author's intentions in the text. Gregor's traumatic change lasts for approximately two days, a pivotal time in his life. At the start of his first day he resembles Joseph Bloch in *Angst*: he becomes neurotically obsessed with the details and objects of the outer world. Like Bloch's, Gregor's alienation is characterized by "seeing" too much and the inability to conceptualize. His behavior is outwardly normal, though inwardly different. Walking along a sidewalk in Paris, he reads, written in chalk, "*Oh la belle vie*"; underneath it is the mysterious statement that the writer is "like you" (*Stunde*, 23). Gregor writes down the phone number included with this message, which he interprets as a sign specifically intended for himself. He makes an appointment with the stranger, the writer of the message. Signs and signals come at him from everywhere. His field of vision swarms with "clear spots." Getting out of a city bus, he is motionless, trying to focus on something, like the sky. Somebody, a stranger, tells him everything is "normal." For Gregor, "normality" acquires a painful meaning.

Gregor's plunge into absurdity as a result of his dream leads directly into textual imagery of the atavistic behavior that is so characteristic of alienated experience: "He felt a taste of blood in his mouth. What repulsed him was not that one night had changed him but that everything else continued to be the same. He didn't look the same but others did" (*Stunde*, 36-37). Gregor's sexuality in the novel is especially allied to eruptions of inner violence. He is obsessed with signals of sexual invitation and conquest. His "obscene" face is exposed to any woman. He wonders whether he should be in a park, next to a clump of bushes (*Stunde*, 36).

Handke's finely tuned analysis of Gregor's alienation includes not only an incisive portrait of a man adrift within a self-generating system of dislocation but also the revelation that this is moving Gregor forward, creating its own life-saving level of new consciousness. This new level will become the means by which Gregor regains a different, self-defined world, free of alienation, where fear becomes for him an important first step in self-evaluation.

An important example of such renewal occurs in a key passage: Gregor, fearful of returning home to his wife and in dread of having to pretend he wants to see her and the child, enters a park and sits on a bench, depressed at the prospect of another domestic confrontation. In a blaze of mystical insight, and experiencing complete silence in his head for the first time that day, Gregor sees three objects at his feet: a piece of a pocket mirror, a child's barrette, and a chestnut leaf. Stripped of their anonymity, they turn into miraculous objects, sublime mysteries for Gregor. They put him into a confident, peaceful mood, an augury of Handke's "moment of true feeling." Gregor further reflects that he has not discovered a mystery in those objects uniquely intended for himself. He believes he has found something valuable, the *idea* of a mystery to which all can relate. Names can function not only as concepts but as ideas (*Stunde*, 82). These three objects, visualized by Gregor in the guise of ideas rather than named objects, seem to signal life-saving themes of discovery and renewal within the predictable pattern of his life. Potentiality predicates possibility, the portal to the realm of a "true moment of feeling." This moment in the park is a turning point in the text, and Handke never intended for it to be apprehended on a realistic level. In his interview with Heinz Ludwig Arnold, Handke remarked that the "moment" is a fantastic instance of "consolation" and "peace," inspired by his reading of fairy tales, in which the hero might see "on the floor of a forest three magical things. . . . These promise to give him happiness, insight, peace and mystery" (29). The moment is actually a natural ending to Gregor's bizarre day, the not unexpected conclusion to the activities of a man rendered helpless by a loss of control. The moment is also Gregor's brief glimpse into the possibility of harmony between the objective (things) and subjective (himself) phases of his environment. As Linstead has noted, however, this episode functions in a similar way to that of Gregor's dream of himself as a murderer at the beginning of the text (1988, 16).[7] Both Gregor's three objects and his opening dream are used by Handke to portend "possibility" and even liberation from alienated experience. In this sense, they are fortuitous events whose timing in the novel is both necessary and predictable.

Gregor's second day begins ominously with his wife's departure. Her last words to him are ambiguous but directed only to himself, since they seem to describe his personal crisis. She tells him that he cannot hope to ask her to give him the meaning of his life. This ironic yet instructive message from Stefanie is actually in line with those episodes of the text that register change and hope for Gregor. The reader, for example, might have felt that Stefanie, as Gregor's wife, was a prime factor in his alienation; yet her departure will force him to reorder and redirect his personal life, and her absence will move him out of senseless existence. Left alone with his daughter in an empty apartment, Gregor is restless and tries to fit the child and himself into a plan that can help them survive. Young Agnes, however, needs no preformulated structure of daily activity. Like the dream that signaled the onset of change in Gregor's life, caring for Agnes becomes a learning process and a new departure point for Gregor. What he gets from Agnes is a gift freely given by the daughter to her father: naïveté, independence, and the absence of moral judgment. She is destined, however, to leave his life. At one point, just as Gregor is about to lose her in a crowd of passersby at a city square, both are resting on a bench. Handke relates here pertinent yet changing aspects of Gregor's new insight into his daughter's role as a vehicle for hope and renewal. He senses his daughter's trust while speaking to him. She reveals something of her inner self, especially her secrets. He is happy that she has secrets! He notes that she uses language like his own. She sees the shapes of nature: clouds, trees and puddles of water (*Stunde*, 144).

As Agnes runs off to play with other children, Gregor resumes reading a passage from a novel of Henry James, and it is at this moment that the child disappears. This loss occurs when her physical presence in Gregor's life is most desirable. Losing Agnes, how-

ever, though in reality only a temporary phenomenon, corresponds
with the novel's message inasmuch as it is a positive sign that the
"old" Gregor must learn to accept his status as a bachelor. The loss
of the child helps him to understand the nature of loss itself, especially among the masses around him. He had lost contact with other
people's feelings and sentiments. Misery and despair mingle with
kindness and empathy. "Nothing seemed to be foolish" (*Stunde*,
148). These lines indicate Gregor's reentry into the social community. Sights and sounds start to matter, and Gregor wants nothing
more for himself, only to watch and observe the crowd moving about
him with self-generating energy. The following passage describes
well the rebirth of life and vitality within Gregor as he emerges from
his submersion in alienation and disorientation: "The usual things
shone before his eyes, as though they were 'appearances' – natural
ones, and such appearance showed him a plenitude that was inex-
haustible . . . it now seemed to him that the idea coming to him in
the Carré Marigny, when he saw the three objects in the sand, was
indeed workable and viable" (*Stunde*, 151-52).

In the last paragraph of the text Handke literally changes the
novel's narrative point of view. He moves away from the subjectivity
of Gregor's consciousness ("I") to an objective consciousness
("he"); the reader "sees" Gregor presented as "the hero of an
unknown tale" – that is, a fictional other man, crossing the Place de
l'Opéra, eager to keep his telephone date with the unknown woman
whose telephone number he had found randomly on the sidewalk
the previous day. He has bought a new suit, socks, and shoes. He is
mentally and emotionally a free man. His daughter has been
reclaimed by her mother. A new Gregor emerges from the false
chrysalis of an unhappy, alienated life.

Stunde is an important book in Handke's ongoing narrative
study of contemporary alienated experience. It offers an interesting
insight into alienated behavior and the subsequent resolution of that
experience through the means of an epiphany, a "true moment of
feeling." The novel defends that moment as a point of entry into
inner harmony, into a quasi-religious sense of contentment. Gregor
feels free to reinvent his life and become the subject of a new life.
This possibility, the reader finds out, most certainly contains elements of mystical harmony and confrontation with the mysteries of
illogic itself. *Stunde*, while offering no tangible evidence that Gre-

gor's change will be permanent, is nevertheless plausible philosophically, and it is a successful rendering of a dialectic concerned with the resolution of alienated conflict engendered by contemporary social experience. Highly subjective in its point of view, *Stunde* sacrifices plot and character development, two dependencies of the traditional novel, as it expresses the ineffable as well as contemporary alienated experience and Gregor's way out of it into affirmative existence. In the end Handke is content to abandon Kafka's and even Sartre's sense of "no exit" from the protypical existentialist state. Thus, *Stunde*, while inspired by notions of contemporary alienation in modern fiction, appends a different solution to that experience. Therein lies its originality.

Die linkshändige Frau

Handke's next novel, *Die linkshändige Frau* (The Left-handed woman), was published in Germany in 1976, one year before the author directed it as a feature film.[8] In the film the veteran stage actress Edith Cleaver plays the role of the woman, and Bruno Graz, a familiar face in new German cinema, is her husband. Cleaver and Graz, who have performed together at the Schaubühne am Halleschen Ufer theater in Berlin, are respected figures in European theatrical and film circles. They appear in French director Erich Rohmer's 1976 film adaptation of Heinrich von Kleist's classic German novella, *Die Marquise von O . . .* (1806). American reviews of Handke's film were enthusiastic: "rhythmically tuned and visually talented" (*Village Voice*); "daring . . . sustained with the high confidence of art" (*New Yorker*).[9] The film was released during the apex of the revival of German art cinema in the United States. Handke had already contributed two scripts for Wim Wenders's film adaptations of *Angst* and *Falsche Bewegung* (1974; Wrong movement), the latter a rendering of Goethe's mammoth novel *Wilhelm Meisters Lehrjahre* (1821-29), so he was prepared to direct his own feature film.[10] As a film, *Frau* incorporates Handke's tributes to masters of Italian and Japanese cinema, notably, Michelangelo Antonioni and Yasujiro Ozu, whose work Handke admires.[11] These tributes occur in extended camera shots, focusing on certain objects, that function as cinematic equivalents of narrative prose and convey subtle feelings of alienation and disorientation related to the portrait of Handke's central character, the "left-handed woman."

Handke made no important narrative changes in the film adaptation of *Frau*. The novel (131 pages in its German edition) betrays
definite signs of its origins as an intended screenplay: an episodic
structure; outdoor imagery; a directorial emphasis on gesture and
movement as elements of setting and place. Handke's novel is an
outstanding example of the ongoing esthetic relationship between
novel writing and film adaptation.

In May 1978 Handke wrote an informative essay, "Durch eine
Mythische Tür eintreten," that sheds light on the film adaptation, as
well as on his intentions in writing the novel.[12] Handke recalls the
lingering image of a male figure, living a contented but lonely existence, feeding his cat and playing chess with himself. This image was
changed in the writing of his prose text into that of a solitary woman,
who in Handke's mind became an artistic analogue to the man. Like
her male counterpart, she succeeds in finding peace at the end of
personal conflict ("Mythische Tür," 234). Handke claims that it was
his intention in the book to show the woman as a survivor, with her
pride and dignity intact: "Since it's a rule that a single woman is
abandoned, I wanted to create a woman who, though tired and
worn out, remains untouchable, like Marlowe in Chandler's novels"
("Mythische Tür," 234). After writing *Wunschloses Unglück*, the
biography of his mother's life and suicide, depicting her as a victim
of conservative social and historical forces, he had decided to tell the
story anew, with a protagonist who would emerge as a heroine of
everyday life. Like Handke's mother, the woman would have experienced social pressures and conformity, but in contrast to his mother,
she would survive to bear witness to her travail. If she desired, she
would be content to play chess by herself. Handke notes that the
image of a lonely chess player was one of those "very mythical and
peaceful images that inspired the film" ("Mythische Tür," 235).

Marianne, the principal character, lives with her eight-year-old
son and her husband, Bruno, in a German suburb, probably in the
Frankfurt area. In the film, however, the setting is Clamart, a suburb
of Paris, an area where Handke was then living. Bruno is a business
representative who, at the beginning of the book, has returned from
a trip to Finland. On the evening of his arrival Marianne, a model of
domestic contentment, is eager to help her son write an assigned
essay on the theme of a better life. He reads Marianne a few lines of
his essay: He would stay up at night and sleep wherever he chose. In

this life there would be no rain. He would have a few friends. This is obviously a child's ideal, fantasy world reduced to simplicity. There are signs that the woman is reading between the lines of what she hears. She stands up and stares through a side window at an uninspiring view of lifeless nature. Handke notes that she remains submerged in her thoughts. After Bruno's return he decides to take his wife to dinner, wishing to spend the night with her in a hotel. Both of these decisions are entirely his own, and they reflect, in fact, his rigid character. He assumes that his plans define the placid (and submissive) state of their relationship, yet after this "idyllic" night is over, Marianne's first words the next morning are hardly what Bruno expects to hear: "I had an odd idea, actually not an idea, but an 'illumination' [*Erleuchtung*]" (*Frau*, 22-23). She relates that the illumination revealed Bruno's impending separation from her. She asks him to move in with her girlfriend for the next several days. Bruno decides to humor her request that he leave her, and he returns to the hotel to have a cup of coffee.

Marianne begins now to live alone, and she resumes her former work as a translator from French into German. The film shows her translating passages from a named text, Gustave Flaubert's novel *Un Coeur simple* (1877), the central theme of which is the miserable fate of a lonely servant woman, but a similar episode in the printed text of *Frau* is about a woman named Michèle and her expressed unhappiness with marriage. The following excerpt refers to Marianne's unnamed project and cites the lines she is translating. These lines also reflect the interaction in Handke's novel between Marianne's unhappy life with Bruno and literature: "Till now men have weakened me. My husband says that I am strong. He really wants me strong for things that are for him uninteresting: the children, the household, taxes. Yet when it comes to work I would like to do, he stops me. He calls me a dreamer. If dreaming means to be myself, then I want to be a dreamer" (*Frau*, 57).

Marianne is pursued by her publisher, who tries to court her with flowers and champagne. This man is a caricature of the proverbial male on the prowl for an available woman. He "knows" she is alone because he read the letter she sent him as a plea from a lonely woman. The letter is actually an inquiry about future employment as a translator. The publisher, however, is only one of several males in the text made laughable as a result of Marianne's evolving skill at moving adroitly in a male-dominated world. When she visits her husband's office in the city, she and her son witness Bruno's absurd demonstration of power control. A high point of the visit is his "power stare" (*Macht-Starren*); Marianne and the child can only look at him. Once again Marianne is the observer, rather than the doer, of activity that defines reality under masculine control.

As Schlueter has noted, the text of *Frau* challenges the rhetoric of feminist sexual politics (1981, 149). And as Mixner and Eberhard Frey have noted, it would be misleading to read the book as a political tract pleading its case for female independence because Marianne lives alone.[13] Handke's understanding of Marianne is shown especially in those episodes concerned with her friend Franziska, a schoolteacher and Bruno's current lover. Franziska invites Marianne to join a consciousness-raising feminist group, ostensibly to learn how she can live as a woman undeceived by a man.

Franziska, the group's leader, never learns that Marianne has observed the group in secret and made a decision not to become a member. Her reasons are entirely private and are not given in the text, yet they seem to be grounded in a conviction that feminist group therapy is less effective than talking to oneself. Franziska also arranges a visit from Marianne's father, and when he arrives he predicts a life of loneliness for his daughter, one similar to his own. He confesses that he is involved in a loveless relationship with an older woman, because he is lonely, yet he chooses to live with the deception that he loves her. Marianne becomes a "left-handed woman," attractive to other solid nonconformists. Sitting alone in the living room of her home, Marianne listens to a song that alludes to her condition: the singer mentions a "face in the crowd," the one exceptional woman in the human mass on a city street. He "sees" her at an office building, or standing alone, reading papers posted on a wall. The woman in the song is a symbol of Handke's Marianne, an eccentric solitary, one who dares to be different. At this point in the text Handke blends musical and narrative images, as a counterpoint to one another, so that the words of this song explicate the deeper meaning of Marianne's independence. Earlier in the novel Handke had used Marianne's translated French novel for similar purposes. Her role as a diffident person out of step with the general mood of society is apparent. She follows her own program of inner renewal and moves to the beat of a different drummer.

At the end of the novel is a spontaneous party at Marianne's house that includes Bruno and Franziska; Marianne's publisher and his chauffeur; an unnamed actor in love with Marianne; and a sales-girl from a local shop. Most of these people have entered Marianne's simple life as a friend, stranger, or potential lover. They are as adrift in the world as she. Each guest arrives with his or her own agenda: reconciliation, love, sympathy, or human understanding. For a time, barriers are dropped and compassion becomes the order of the evening. Even Franziska, who walks through the door with Bruno, says half-seriously to Marianne that they expected to find a very lonely woman. The party functions as Handke's narrative device that shows the reader an uninhibited episode of life, one deeply affective in its sensitive transitory beauty. Sadness and anger at the human condition are exchanged for brief glimpses into moments of true feeling. The reader waits for the euphoria and goodwill to disappear and may be put off by the apparent frivolity. Simple activities like dancing and drinking champagne with strangers become occasions for personal empathy and confession. Given names are used and exchanged. Though Marianne's fate as a single woman is the com-mon thread, it is Franziska who delivers one of the novel's most compelling definitions of loneliness: it is the pain of "unreality," a suffering relieved by the presence of other people (*Frau*, 120).

Handke's narration in this episode is primarily conveyed through simple, placid gestures and movements. Some of these are unex-pected: dice throwing, nail cutting, and even drawing. Vindictive behavior is obviated. Professional and class barriers are dropped. The publisher and salesgirl dance with one another. The chauffeur, with a glass of champagne in his hand, goes about toasting his "friends." For a moment Handke's quasi-pastoral setting gives the reader a vision of life in peaceful, languid simplicity. Bruno's child even asks his father to play with him. The salesgirl, relieved briefly from the tension and stress of work as a public drudge, continues to dance with the publisher and starts to play dice with Marianne's child. Bruno, on the other hand, ends up cutting his son's nails in the bathroom (*Frau*, 118). There are also incidents of clever male pursuit of women, rendered, however, in an amusing, erotic way; Handke deliberately holds back from direct psychological portrayal. A cinematic, elliptical narrative style predominates. Frey, an early reviewer of the novel, noted, "This [technique] makes for fascinating

reading because we are constantly challenged to interpret the
actions and conversations and to understand what must be going on
in [Marianne's] mind" (608). If the reader never actually perceives
the full context of Marianne's thoughts, Handke sometimes shows
his meaning in several revealing lines of the text. Standing alone
before a mirror at the end of the party, Marianne says, "You didn't
betray yourself. You'll never be humiliated again" (*Frau*, 130). Her
words, however, are more than the security of pride and integrity.
These lines are important because they reveal a conviction of her
inner self, and without this conviction coming through as strongly as
it does Marianne would be only a neurotic or a poser. The question
never arises. We now realize that Handke has orchestrated the party
episode to show us Marianne, who has become an observer of others, emerging as a woman gaining control of herself and her environment, experiencing a sense of inner balance and equilibrium. She
begins to make a space for herself, and even her former husband
admires her independence.

Schlueter, however, has said that the novel can be read as "a
study in solitude" that emphasizes Marianne's return to primordial
consciousness, a "natural joy," perhaps a state of being beyond the
concerns of an adult world (1981, 152). I favor this reading. Other
readers, noting Handke's narrative skill at writing a text that is neither a feminist tract nor a political allegory, choose to stress the
poetic and mythical quality of the book, especially the elusive particularity of Marianne itself. Handke deconstructs Marianne's identity
throughout as a wife and a woman. Her name is only indirectly mentioned in the text. She is usually referred to abstractly as "the
woman." Her identity then derives from a pair of opposites: man-
wife. Opposite concepts are dominant structural devices in the
novel: winter-spring, light-dark, nature-city. Marianne's specificity is
depersonalized, and Handke intentionally moves her in the direction
of generality, perhaps of myth. Quoted in an article in *Der Spiegel*
written during the filming, Handke stated his wish to create Marianne as a "myth" rather than a realistic woman, thereby suggesting
her potential origins as a creature of his spiritual imagination: "I had
the feeling of entering a mythical door, where the laws governing
other lives had disappeared."[14] Handke has indeed chosen to endow
Marianne's character with the aura of spirituality. It turns out later

that sexuality has nothing to do with her reasons for separating from her husband.

Marianne's plan to separate from Bruno is a decision that sets her on a path predicated by inner wisdom. Her rebirth as a woman is within the context of a growing spirituality. As a prototype, Marianne functions at first in a nameless place, a modern, anonymous suburban setting that becomes alive only through the regeneration of her spiritual self, when she can summon the vitality to live alone and her eyes are opened to nature and the environment. Marianne's sense of inner control moves in tandem with her exposure to nature, as Handke shows in the text: for example, in the party episode, when she is looking out a window and the tops of trees are moving about, she is reawakened into nature and life (*Frau*, 121); a long climb up a mountain with her child is an occasion for the rebirth of sensitivity and closeness between Marianne and the child. The vision of nature from above the city inspires memory to function between them. They have a tranquil day (*Frau*, 105). Marianne's reawakening coincides with her sensitivity to nature and is especially allied to a rebirth of an inner health-giving process of peace and security.

Mixner insists that Marianne's quest for identity remains an unsolvable mystery, beyond the reach of rational explanation or even of a code revealed through a metalanguage, the language of hidden meaning within the text. "The author's language," Mixner notes, "is that of poetry, and writing poetry contains both its own goal and its own meaning. The mythical level of the novel shows the reader that the goal of Handke's poetry is self-knowledge and inner experience" (231). Like Keuschnig in *Stunde*, Marianne is a creature who falls out of the realm of the everyday into the context of poetry. But her fate can only end in a context of silence.

If the final image of Gregor in *Stunde* is that of a man sporting a fictive persona, a man content to physically wear another set of clothes, the closing scenes of *Frau* are very different. Peace and tranquillity surround a solitary Marianne, sitting in the living room of her house, her legs propped on a chair, a glass of whiskey in her hand. She begins to draw, first her feet, then the objects in the room around her. If she is awkward and uncertain, she still manages to do a line in one movement. Her drawing is analogous to her tentative but determined insight into the meaning of her new life.

Drawing is a silent art, and highly revelatory to the artist. Drawing need not be dependent on words for its execution and performance. Marianne's act of drawing as an act of identity is followed by
a short closing scene in which she sits alone on the terrace of her
house. If this woman realizes inner freedom and a release from outer
conflict, then it is in the nature of a limited and valuable gift of
"selective withdrawal" – that is, the possibility of flight into the
peace of an asocial world (Schlueter 1981, 152). In retrospect, her
recent life as a single woman has become a spiritual adventure in
inner wisdom, resulting in a freedom that has allowed her to flee her
restrictive roles as housewife, wife, and mother at the age of 30.
Empathy, compassion, and detachment, if not understanding, for a
unique life-style are memorable aspects of Handke's book that make
it a relevant spiritual text to a sympathetic reader.

Chapter Five

Recent Developments: A Tetralogy

A New Stylistic Effort

Four separate texts make up a Handke tetralogy published from 1979 to 1981. Three works in the tetralogy are known collectively in English as *Slow Homecoming*.[1] Unified by the homecoming theme, they stress Handke's shift as a creative writer from linguistic analysis to the broader themes of the redemptive and connective aspects of nature, art, parenting, and communal life. *Langsame Heimkehr* (1979; The Long way around) is the title of the first text in this group, and its protagonist is a scientist.[2] The second title, *Die Lehre der Sainte-Victoire* (1980; The Lesson of Mont Sainte-Victoire) is a semi-autobiographical account of Handke's esthetics and features an unnamed writer's analysis of Paul Cézanne's paintings of Mont Sainte-Victoire in the south of France.[3] In *Sainte-Victoire* the writer undertakes a walking trip in the region where Cézanne actually finished his paintings of the mountain. Klinkowitz and Knowlton note that both *Heimkehr* and *Sainte-Victoire* "work to subvert the perniciously antihumanist progress of science and scientific thought – geology plays an important role in both books – by proposing a synthesis of twentieth-century positivism with the idealism of a past era" (94). The last two works in the tetralogy, *Kindergeschichte* (1981; Child story) and *Über die Dörfer* (1981; Through the villages) focus on the spirituality of childhood and communal existence.[4] The homecoming theme of the tetralogy thus incorporates nature, fatherhood and the timeless existence of Austrian village life. The sequential and autobiographical works of the tetralogy are of substantial interest for those readers who wish to penetrate confessional aspects of Handke's life.

In 1979 Handke remarked about the tetralogy to Schlueter:

I can only say I have expanded myself as never before within this writing. It is
an attempt to reach a world harmony and at the same time to reach a universality for myself as someone who writes, an attempt which may have been too
daring – sometimes this is so in the narrative – or in this epic poem, as you
will surely call it. Because of what happened forty or so years ago [World War
II], we have no more power for beauty; no one can really live the right way
here, and there is no nature, or there is nature, but no language for nature,
what Hölderlin speaks of as the great nature. (1981, 176-77)

Primary words in the passage above are "world harmony," "epic
poem," "beauty," "language for nature," and "great nature." The
subjectivity of these words, some of them open borrowings from
German romantic literature, is striking, yet they point the way toward
which any critical analysis of the works of the tetralogy must move.
The interview shows Handke as a seer and a healer of discord and
alienation. He allies beauty to harmony (almost a classical reference), and his phrase "language for nature" leads him to speak at
length about poetic language. What he says on this subject can be
related to the language and style of the tetralogy in general:
"[Language] is a very valuable proof of life. . . . There is almost no
language any more. It is only when I live and have a feeling that there
is a future that language appears, not only for me as a writer. . . .
Most people have no language at all. There is a sigh of relief through
the masses when there is someone who has a language. What is this
language? I believe this language is only poetic language. . . . The
only thing which is valid for me, where I feel very
powerful – powerful without power – is when I succeed in finding
form with language" (1981, 173).

Handke's tetralogy was written under the thematic and artistic
influences of Hölderlin, the early-nineteenth-century German poet.
In this same interview Handke asserts that Hölderlin "writes a holy
scripture, in a completely objective sense. . . . I had not understood
him before. But now I can read his work as a far better written and
morally highstanding, holy scripture, where one is not forced to believe, but because sentences stand like mountain ranges, can simply
believe, or at least see an ideal" (1981, 174).

Several of Handke's recent critics have observed that the tetralogy represents a new thematic and stylistic effort in the author's lit-

erary odyssey.[5] Though still analytical, he no longer desires to "perish" in linguistic analysis. Texts such as *Frau, Stunde,* and *Das Gewicht der Welt* also signaled changes in his language and thematic direction. An alert reader of *Gewicht* (a journal) will note its subjective, perceptive entries about nature, art, and history and about the need to reinvent myth in order to understand nature. Instead of Handke's familiar posture as a linguistic innovator, as in *Publikumsbeschimpfung, Kaspar,* and *Bodensee,* his mentors in the tetralogy are the founding fathers of German classical fiction: Goethe, Gottfried Keller and Adalbert Stifter. Major characters in each of the four texts reflect different aspects of Handke's search for the "law-giving moment" of natural phenomena, a law that links man most directly to the totality of the environment. This law will heal, redeem, and create the modern world anew. Arnold Blumer refers to this law as a paradigmatic example of Handke's turn (at this point) to "Romantic irrationality" and his abandonment of language and political themes for the starry vision of a poetic utopia.[6]

Langsame Heimkehr

Sorger, the main character in *Langsame Heimkehr,* is a quintessential example of Handke's alienated man, a figure already found in the two previous novels, *Angst* and *Stunde.* Sorger is viewed initially against the isolated landscape of the Alaskan Far North. The reader follows his moves to the Bay Area of northern California (Berkeley), and from there to the Denver mountains. He goes eastward to New York City before returning to Europe a wiser and more compassionate man because of everything he has experienced. It is important to note that Sorger (a "worrier") is a recluse and a voluntary exile in the Alaskan wilderness, someone who has chosen his particular lifestyle. Handke describes him as a refugee from the modern maladies of formlessness and fragmentation and notes that his inner life and his work as a geologist are one and the same phenomenon. Ambiguously described as a man without longing but susceptible to facts, Sorger nonetheless finds the formless world of the North a good arena in which to examine and meditate on form and space in his environment. The expansiveness of the Alaskan territories is open to Sorger's common habit of projecting unity and order onto the formless landscape. He thus enjoys a sense of personal control over his subjective creation of bounded spaces, bodies of water, and moun-

tain ranges. Sorger also believes that in Alaska he is struggling successfully against the primitive environment. He thinks that he can
move to heal the split between himself and the outer world of
nature. In a central passage Sorger expresses his confidence that
studying the earth's forms is of great benefit to understanding his
inner self, that it gives him an identity (a form). He can save himself
and a part of the outside world from an undifferentiated "formless"
world (*Heimkehr*, 15-16).

Thus for a time Sorger is successful in overcoming his existential
problems and is able to give order and definition to both the outer
and inner worlds of nature and himself. But Handke proceeds to
criticize this gift as a facile and solipsistic solution to alienation.
Before Sorger leaves Alaska, and preceding his return to California,
Handke sets the stage for Sorger's renewal of self and his reintegra-
tion into society. This occurs within a mystical setting: Sorger has a
presentiment of his future isolation and a forewarning of death if he
does not experience a "change of direction." One evening before his
departure for California he is standing beside a river bed and enters
into a reverie of solitude. He hears the whimpering of an abandoned
child, and "a voice from the darkness issues a cryptic warning . . .
about the dangers of going blind from gazing too long into the snow
[i.e., the Alaskan wilderness]" (Sharp, 225). The voice Sorger hears is
quasi-realistic – it is not clear where it comes from – but it warns
him against an "inward-turning vision" (*Heimkehr*, 81) that will turn
him against his child, still in Europe, and the perilous consequences
of spending his life in a place as anonymous as Alaska. Sorger is thus
reminded that Alaska symbolizes the end of his cultural identity. It is
at this point that he not only decides to leave for California but
begins an unprejudiced search for cohesion and unity in the outer
social world, which he now feels to be a world of potential *human*
dimensions.

In California Sorger's alienated Alaskan "nature world" begins to
fall apart. This can be understood as the beginning of his abandonment of philosophical egocentricity, including his first steps toward
the realm of personal relationships. One such relationship is Sorger's
friendship with his neighbors, a married couple who are Middle
Europeans like himself. Sympathy for other human beings, Sorger
notes, has enhanced their married life; his neighbor's wife seems to
him an exemplary person in her love for the world of others. For

Sorger, his time in California is a key to rediscovering himself in the community of man. He is moved into a confessional mode and the admission that he can no longer live alone. His stop in California, another landscape, is thus a step away from the solipsistic alienation of Alaska. Nature in California, he learns, forbids the luxury of private, individual spaces. From Handke's point of view, this means that the personal spaces of an egocentric like Sorger, devised through the medium of dreams and inversion, must give way to the actual space of people and their cultural setting. This is the meaning of the title of chapter 2, "Raumverbot" (Forbidden space).

Linstead notes that in *Heimkehr* Handke uses natural landscapes as a mirror of Sorger's feelings and emotions (1988, 175). He borrowed this technique from nineteenth-century German prose writers like Novalis, Stifter, and Keller. One thinks also of the related narrative content of the German romantic novella. Sorger's existence has been observed against the landscape settings of Alaska and northern California, first as an alienated man, then as a figure about to undergo a move toward the social realm of action. California and the Berkeley community become the catalysts for Sorger's "personal yet collective" (*Heimkehr*, 133) appropriation of the human landscape, foreshadowing his return to Europe, Austria, and home. Sorger's California neighbors offer him the comfort of sympathetic European fellowship and a reentry into the lost world of European cultural identity.

Sorger goes next to the Denver mountains, ostensibly to visit an old school friend. This visit is a move eastward. When Sorger arrives in Colorado, he reads that his friend is dead. Sorger's grief over his dead friend retrieves the memory of his brother and sister, alone in Europe and "dead" to his affection. As Sorger looks down into the night from a plane heading for New York, he reads "the lights of a town below him" (*Heimkehr*, 159) as cemetery paths or stars leading the way back to the time when Sorger embraced his siblings at the death of his parents. On an autobiographical level, these scenes are allusions to Handke's loss of his mother and his fear of possibly losing other family connections. In this novel Handke is never far from memories and episodes taken from his life in Altenmarkt. Sorger makes a clear decision to return to Europe and Austria.

In New York, during the last stop on his homeward journey, history, time, and healing coalesce into Sorger's "law-giving moment,"

an incident similar to Gregor Keuschnig's in *Stunde*. These several
pages of the novel are mystical and spiritual in tone and inspiration.
In Handke's context, the law-giving moment of *Heimkehr* is analogous to "a moment of true feeling," the "recognition of and orientation within the mutuality of simple existence" (DeMeritt, 61).
Handke calls Sorger's experience an inner vision encompassing "all
those inventions, discoveries, sounds, images, and forms down
through the centuries that make for a possibility of humanity"
(*Heimkehr*, 114). The law-giving moment is also Sorger's
reassessment of the history that is unique to himself as a
contemporary European. He learns that history is not a mere
chronology of evil. In his reassessment of historical time, Handke
stresses the potentiality of present and future history. Sorger thus
becomes the "subject" of future history, not its past record. Sorger is
thankful that he can learn to live in harmony with the course of
unencumbered, normative history. The unbridled formlessness of
European history hinges on guilt. During this epiphany, Sorger turns
away from thoughts focused only on his personal salvation. Handke
notes that the coffee shop table where Sorger sits resembles the
surface of the earth. The city becomes a metaphor for "a vitalistic,
living organ" (*ein mächtiger lebendig Naturkörper*) (*Heimkehr*,
171). Sorger's new perception of nature is thus revitalized to
incorporate human dimensions, including himself as an active
participant in nature's business.

As if to demonstrate this new change, Sorger's chance meeting
with a fellow Austrian, someone in dire need of help, reinforces his
sense of rebirth and regeneration. Before Sorger returns to Europe,
he will first counsel the man and help him overcome his self-accusation and guilt. Sorger at first has the impression that he is listening to
his own story and witnessing the absurdity of his former life. This
time, however, he manages to retreat from the utter hopelessness of
the stranger's tale. He becomes the ideal "outside observer," redi-
recting unhappiness and suffering into harmonious order. He plays
the role of a sympathetic audience well (*Heimkehr*, 174-75).

Heimkehr, so replete with visions of nature, first under the illusion of personal control through form, space, and time and then
changed under Sorger's emerging structures of social culture and
history, reveals that nature is a metaphor for the human dimensions
of life. Sorger reassesses his life. What began as a hymn to the

wilderness of the far North as the ultimate place of refuge from a fragmented world concludes as a vision of possible harmony and unity, a rescue from alienation. Along the way Handke functions as the great orchestrator of "harmony and beauty to serve as a counterweight to the existing world's banality" (Klinkowitz and Knowlton, 90). Subsequent texts of the tetralogy continue this and allied themes, demonstrating the widening breadth of Handke's literary esthetics and natural philosophy.

Die Lehre der Sainte-Victoire

Mont Sainte-Victoire is the name of a mountain in the south of France that was the subject of a series of Cézanne's late paintings. A commentator on Cézanne writes,

> As Cézanne experimented with the theme of Mont Sainte-Victoire – to which he returned no fewer than sixty times – the panorama became less and less complex and the melodic line more and more discreet while space was expressed in an increasingly intellectual manner. . . . The further Cézanne progressed in this series, the less attention he paid to the rules of perspective . . . gradually the background becomes more important than the foreground and the famous mountain comes nearer. . . . Eventually, the landscape becomes simply a symphony of wild splashes of color and moving shapes, which lead the spectator by slow stages to the heart of the geological drama, right to the undefined core, where apparent and imagined reality are one.[7]

Though it emulates a nonfiction work, Handke's *Die Lehre der Sainte-Victoire* is hard to classify, for it is both an esthetic text and a prose narrative. It has an unnamed narrator (Sorger-Handke) who, at the beginning of the book, describes the initial impact of Cézanne's paintings upon his writing. At one point the narrator says that reading Adalbert Stifter's novella *Bergkristall* (1852) led him directly to "colors" – that is, to examine color in prose. He went to a Cézanne exhibition in the spring of 1978. The use of color in Cézanne's work struck him as a possible new beginning for his own quest for a renewal of prose writing. He was as inspired by Cézanne as he had been by Flaubert. For Cézanne, color and form were enough to enable the painter to "realize" his subject.

The narrator-writer of *Sainte-Victoire* ("I") shifts into an especially autobiographical mode whenever the book's discussion moves toward esthetics, a personal experience. *Sainte-Victoire* contains memories of Handke's childhood in rural Austria, where, he notes, paintings were found only in the parish church. Handke recounts episodes from his life in Paris and gives his recollections of living in Berlin at the end of World War II. He reveals that Slovene was his first language, as well as other interesting details about about familial connections to Germany and Slovenia. *Sainte-Victoire* suggests that Sorger's character in *Heimkehr* was derived from a portrait in the 1978 Cézanne exhibition, specifically, a painting called *Hommes aux bras croisés* (*Sainte-Victoire*, 36-37). If Sorger is portrayed by Handke as a geologist who abandons science to expand his human and cultural consciousness, the narrator-writer of *Sainte-Victoire* reflects the next step in Handke's ongoing dialogue with the discovery of new connections between himself and the outer world. In a comparison of *Heimkehr* and *Sainte-Victoire*, Klinkowitz and Knowlton have noted that *Sainte-Victoire* mirrors Handke's special concern with things and objects, with "relinking . . . the outerworld and the innerworld as a mystical unity" capable of saving objects "from the threat of transience" (92). In *Sainte-Victoire*, as opposed to *Heimkehr*, Handke proposes Cézanne's esthetics as a means to "secure" alienated objects of the material world. These objects, lost to the narrator-writer through estrangement, alienation, and meaningless language, are reformulated by Handke in *Sainte-Victoire* in terms of Cézanne's *réalisation*. This realization is perhaps best understood as a harmony of unity and peace, the resolution of contradictions in a state of innocence. Like Handke himself in an earlier phase of artistic development – one recalls his esthetics in the *Sprechstücke* – the narrator of *Sainte-Victoire* refers to Cézanne's victory as an artist over alienation and estrangement. He notes that Cézanne first painted horror pictures (*Schreckensbilder*) but later turned to the "realization" of earth's innocence: an apple, a cliff, or a human face. For Cézanne, form became identical with reality (*Sainte-Victoire*, 21).

Structurally, the first part of *Sainte-Victoire* begins as a flashback. The narrator refers to a pivotal time in his creative life – during his return to Europe – when he underwent a transition from an untenable stage of comprehending reality to a "higher" level of esthetic and spiritual freedom. He was for the first time comfortable with colors in the panorama of human experience. Nature's world and man's world conspired ecstatically to create images and moments of peace and totality, something that Handke calls *Nunc stans* (a unity of eternity) (*Sainte-Victoire*, 9-10).

The narrator sets the beginning of this epiphany in the country-side of Aix-en-Provence and the village of Le Tholonet in southern France. These were actually Cézanne's natural surroundings as a painter in his last years. The narrator recalls his reasons, both intri-cate and deliberate, for making this journey in Cézanne's footsteps: (a) his lingering interest in the history of art, including figures like Jean Courbet, René Magritte, and Edward Hopper; (b) his focus on the "special effects" of objects in paintings; and (c) his tendency to apprehend life and commonplace things as "dream images." This last reason is connected to the narrator's sense of alienation and disori-entation, whereby dreaming had become a device to avoid outer reality itself. Dreaming became, paradoxically, the narrator-writer's way to apprehend the true reality of things and objects. A dreamer, however, comes to rely on his dreams, confusing those dreams with life. The narrator admits that "relative" or dream imagery as a basis for his art ruined his writing and his reentry into life. Fearing there-fore that alienation would continue to deconstruct his world of objective reality, the narrator is now ready to move into a new sys-tem of esthetics. He confesses his need for a teacher, and this teacher will be Cézanne.

The second major part of *Sainte-Victoire* relates the way the narrator-writer comes to accept Cézanne's greatness as a teacher. First the reader is asked to accept the esthetic and spiritual impact of Cézanne's subject (Mont Sainte-Victoire) on the narrator himself: he perceives that the mountain became the object from which Cézanne painted "reasonable" pictures, which differ from the artist's earlier ones in that their reasonableness derives from unity, not alienation, between subject and object (DeMeritt, 63). The narrator, however, has never been able to produce anything in prose analogous to Cézanne's reasonable landscapes of Mont Sainte-Victoire. In an ideal prose, the narrator feels, there would be no destruction of content for the sake of unity, no disorientation in the subject. The narrator of *Sainte-Victoire* feels impelled "to realize the essence of an object in Cézanne's manner" (DeMeritt, 64). His goal is to compose "objects" in prose as Cézanne united color and form in painting. On Handke's sense of connection between the esthetic perceptions in his art and in Cézanne's, Klinkowitz and Knowlton observe, "Through

Cézanne's art, Handke attempts to break out of the strictures of his individuality and to experience directly the world of objects, bypassing the customary mediation of language and conceptual analysis – just as Cézanne painted through his perceptual notions to capture once more a living sense of the real" (92).

The text of *Sainte-Victoire* attempts to verbalize the narrator's reception of Cézanne's esthetics by stressing the value of Cézanne's direct, immediate association between objects and their colors, thereby allowing the use of the names of these objects both specifically and concretely, avoiding the abstraction of metaphorical language. Like Cézanne, the narrator longs to name objects as a sign of his newfound freedom with those objects. He avoids dwelling on the functions and relationships between objects in his new process of naming. In a key passage in *Sainte-Victoire*, Handke recalls Cézanne's visit to an exhibition of Courbet's paintings at the Louvre. Cézanne, looking at colors, actually called out names for the objects he recognized – hounds, blood, a tree, gloves (*Sainte-Victoire*, 33). Here the narrator states that, for Cézanne, Courbet's objects and their colors were each a separate unity. Cézanne "realized" these objects in their singular unity of color and form. For Handke, realization links a writer's words to their objects without suffering a sense of predetermined meaning brought about through alienation or estrangement. In the penultimate chapter, Handke's narrator articulates his wish to say something further about Sainte-Victoire, Cézanne's mountain. This communication, the "lesson" of Mont Sainte-Victoire, occurs at the end of the narrator's second journey to the mountain, when "suddenly, as if struck by a great force, he imagines himself inside the fissure (of the mountain) and the fissure inside himself" (Klinkowitz and Knowlton, 93). The fissure had always been a visual barrier to the narrator, since it prevented unity and wholeness between himself and the mountain, an obstacle to understanding Cézanne's very concept of realization. Handke's narrator-writer, in a moment of unity between himself and the mountain fissure, sees "the kingdom of words open itself along with the Great Spirit of Form" (*Sainte-Victoire*, 115) – that is, he realizes his creative ability to seize, describe, and articulate the experience of unity in the particular and the universal. The narrator has undergone a *Nunc stans* experience. Mont Sainte-Victoire is no longer a mountain with a fault but a "unified" object.

The narrator's mystical episode would become the basis for Handke's future writing and the structure for his new esthetics. The last chapter of *Sainte-Victoire*, "The Great Forest," is a practical example of the lesson of Mont Sainte-Victoire. This forest, whose name comes from a painting by Jakob van Ruisdael, corresponds to a forest outside Salzburg, near Handke's home. The forest is linked to color and form and mythological sensibility. The trees are dark. At one point the forest seems to spin. At the end of the chapter the narrator notices the remaining stones of a Roman road, linking the forest to the historical past. A common woodpile of sawed "circles," the ends of the cut pieces of wood, shows both color and form to the narrator's vision. These colors contain the footprints of the first man (*des ersten Menschen*) (*Sainte-Victoire*, 138-39).

Sainte-Victoire, like *Heimkehr*, is a key text in Handke's tetralogy not only because he explains the shift in the direction of his prose and novel writing but because the homecoming it celebrates is that of a new artistic perception, one free of alienation and estrangement. His new prose esthetic is built on direct experience and realization, inspired by Cézanne.

Kindergeschichte

Handke's third book in the *Heimkehr* tetralogy is *Kindergeschichte*, a new part of Handke's program of creative and artistic renewal. The autobiographical narrative of the text concerns Handke's paternal relationship with his young daughter, Amina. The text is an episodic record of the 10-year period in which the responsibility of his daughter's rearing and education had fallen almost exclusively on him. *Kindergeschichte* begins with the narrator recounting his youthful dreams of having a child and a family. If one takes this narrator to be Handke himself, then he is expressing sorrow and dismay over his own childhood in Altenmarkt and his adult wish to "rectify" the unhappiness he remembers in his own family (*Kindergeschichte*, 7).

The narrator's dream of the past also contained two other wishes: a woman, and a career that would give life meaning and dignity. The entire text of *Kindergeschichte* is the author's examination of the reasons this threefold dream was destined to fail and why only the father and the child (Handke and Amina) survived the dream. *Kindergeschichte* notes the growing separation between Handke and his wife, Libgart, that preceded the birth of Amina. The roots of this nascent conflict are rendered in emotional language. With Amina's birth the crisis that lay in the making moved on to the level of distrust and recrimination. In *Kindergeschichte* Handke says that before the child was born he had known problems, had been at odds with his wife. They were not suited for one another. Living together was a lie (*Lüge*), and his original dream of a life with a woman was nothing (*eine Nichtigkeit*). Amina's arrival was the catalyst for the breakup (*Kindergeschichte*, 13).

The dissension led the couple into an obsessive pattern of changing residences, before Handke decided to build a home in Kronberg, a new suburb of Frankfurt, where he made an ill-starred endeavor to live amicably with his wife. After this failure, when Amina was five years old, Handke went back to "the beloved foreign city" of Paris (where the family had lived before) to build a life without his wife. Libgart returned to the theater and resumed her career. *Kindergeschichte* highlights those later, solitary years in Paris and gives Amina's story as much as Handke's, as the reader soon finds out. Libgart remains a shadowy figure in the book. The second Paris stay became a time when Handke directed and guided the educational development of his child.[8]

In *Kindergeschichte* Handke never refers to Amina or himself by name; Amina is "the child" and he is "the adult." Both child and adult are thus removed, even alienated, from the reader's attempt to enter the text as autobiography. Handke's text and its point of view are intended to serve as a model case of characterization (*Modell*), more an exemplary instance of "instruction" for the reader than a detailed record of a relationship grounded in reality. The tone of the book is perceptive, cognitive, spiritual. Handke's role as an author is clearly paternal and archetypal, as he seeks to place both the child and the father in a realm outside history and beyond the limitations of common society and culture.

Here it is useful to recall Handke's oft-cited entry in *Das Gewicht der Welt*, in which he speaks of his desire to change the idées fixes of individuals (like himself) into the "mythology" of the many (*Gewicht*, 205). Mythology in Handke's writing is often intended as a corrective to contemporary alienation and estrangement; mythology incorporates normative aspects of life along with psychogenesis and image-making, all of which work together to explicate the "law-giving" insight so characteristic of Handke's alienated characters, who, through epiphanies, achieve breakthroughs into mental and psychic freedom. The domestic crisis of *Kindergeschichte*, set off by the mother's departure to continue her professional career, is the first step for the father's "entry into the world of other children, other human beings and perhaps to a new insight about the world itself."[9] The child (Amina) becomes the adult's (Handke's) teacher and allows him to share an intersubjective experience that frees him from alienation and overbearing solitude. The narrator of *Kindergeschichte* stresses that through the glass partition of the hospital room, he "saw" not a newborn child but a complete adult. The father's secret wish to protect her is revelatory; it comes to him when he notes that her "anonymity" as a baby, the lack of uniqueness in her appearance, assured her innocence in his eyes. He begins to form a "conspiracy" between himself and the child, a committed pair against the world. The mother's presence symbolizes a threat to father-child intimacy.

These words suggest that the child's birth was a special event that signaled to the father a test of the child's (and his) survival under adversity. The text presents both child and father as participants in a process that precludes education and culturalization, yet most conflicts in the book arise within the realms of education, culture, and the burden of living in a foreign country – more specifically, within the state and sectarian schools in France and the communes of German cities, which are filled with social reformers and pedogogical experts. Within the time frame of *Kindergeschichte* the child and her father live in the French and West German cultures of the 1970s. In this sense alone, her survival under changing social and political conditions in those cultures would be a source of interest for others besides her father. Renner has pointed out that a generous portion of *Kindergeschichte* is actually Handke's polemic against conventional educational institutions and self-styled experts, leftist theorists who are "nonparents" themselves.[10] Handke criticizes these elements as a malignancy arising from the "spirit of the times" (*Kindergeschichte*, 19). The author's anger seems to reflect his resentment at not being heard and his inability to share the experience of fatherhood with his friends. Handke's earlier conflicts with the literary establishment at the start of his career were suspended after Amina's birth by a new obstacle: the leftist-oriented social innovators who rejected any notion of conventional family life. In

Kindergeschichte Handke states his belief that leftist agitation for political change is inherently right but he could never accept their dogmatism (*das einzige Mögliche*). Handke was ready to redefine the direction of his life on his own terms.

This passage would seem to show that *Kindergeschichte* is also a tale of a man's finding himself as an individual and a father. Paradoxically, there is little attention given to the child's point of view. Only the narrator's wishes and thoughts on the mystical bond of parenthood are given prominence, especially in the aftermath of an episode (at Kronberg?) that occurs one morning when the child is crying and the father is in the cellar clearing out flood water after a heavy rain. Here the reader is asked to understand that the narrator's fatherhood has been put to the litmus test of everyday living, that as a single father (and mother) he had to give up his fixed routine, something he believed he could do but in which he often failed. The flooded basement evolves into such a test when in anger, he strikes the child in the face. He is remorseful over this unfair punishment, which he interprets as his application of a superior but false sense of power and control. He is horrified, yet the occasion transpires into an instance of repentance and understanding between father and child. He notes the child's way of forgiveness, her clear beaming eyes, raising her (and him) above the "world" (*Kindergeschichte*, 54). The pathetic tone of this language is anticipated earlier in the book when the reader is asked to accept the child as an emanation of "light," a tranquil figure with "ageless" eyes (*Kindergeschichte*, 29). Handke's suggestion that the child has the power to transmit forgiveness is therefore not surprising.

This key episode in the book, which would otherwise be so mundane in its immediate resolution, is in fact important for understanding the mythological level of the text. The father and the child communicate with one another not through words but through their eyes (*der Blick*, Sartre's *le regard*), and the father's spiritual and religious connections to the world of his child are first made through her eyes, eyes that he must learn to read in the sense that any reading is a means of insight and knowledge. Renner traces a pattern of visual, wordless gestures between father and child, a primary source of communication that seems to undermine the need for speech in this private, mythological world (143).

The father's return to Paris with the child after the separation from his wife is portrayed as an attempt to save the child from a "tragedy of destruction," which he sees as the consequence of life led within the rules of the "majority" rather than life as it might be. He enrolls the child in a school run by Jews for children of their faith; he hopes that she will learn there a sense of historical tradition, initiation, and a feeling for communal life. This endeavor, however, is a failure; the father admits that, subliminally, he had wanted to identify with the singular destiny and survival of the Jews in the contemporary world. Assimilation and the rules of Jewish society intervene at this point, and the father is asked to withdraw the child from the school on religious grounds. Clearly he has misunderstood the essence of a major religious tradition.

Handke concludes *Kindergeschichte* by pointing out that he never regretted his time spent with Amina; their life together was an attempt to explore the possibility of a utopian existence between father and child. At the end of the text, when Handke notes that the eyes of children transmit an endless spirit of living, it is clear that for him the primary lesson of fatherhood has been a religious one, and that his child has served as a religious teacher. As a father he is destined "forever" to observe and learn from his child, whom he can follow to the end of the world. These moments of meditation cohere and coalesce into a *song (Kindergeschichte*, 136). His time spent as a father with his child, Handke infers, has moved from words, to wordless gestures, to the abstraction of music. There is a short Greek epigraph at the end of *Kindergeschichte* that in a special way illustrates the main points of the homecoming theme in this third book of the *Heimkehr* tetralogy, a coming together of the child-teacher and the adult. In several lines from Pindar's *Olympian Ode*, Iamos receives the gift of prophecy from his father Apollo: "Come here, my child, and enter the hospitable land, following the sound of my voice!"

Über die Dörfer

Über die Dörfer is subtitled "A Dramatic Poem" and is the last text of the *Heimkehr* tetralogy. As of this date, only *Dörfer* has not been published in English translation. The tetralogy's general theme of redemption is carried over to this work, the only one that is not a prose text. Its genre, like the other titles in the series, is unique: it revives a literary form that bridges poetry and drama. *Dörfer* is a drama for reading, poetic in language and with allusions to Greek classical theater. One dramatic technique frequently used in *Dörfer* is the monologue as source of dramatic confrontation and emotional conflicts. A lengthy "retarding" speech at the conclusion of the play's fourth section functions effectively to prevent direct catastrophe as an outcome of dramatic conflict.

Reading *Dörfer*, however, brings to mind the tenuous boundary line between a dramatic poem and a closet drama, especially if the reader's definition of a closet drama is a play designed to be read rather than acted, a work more successful as literature than as drama in performance. *Dörfer* was first staged at the Salzburg Festival on 8 August 1982. Despite sympathy for the play's originality, its reception by critics in such prestigious newspapers as *Die Zeit* and the *Frankfurter Allgemeine Zeitung* was less than favorable.[11] At best, the five-hour play was accepted by the opening-night audience as a curious and eccentric gesture by a highly eccentric artist. At the end of the first performance the Salzburg audience greeted Handke and Wim Wenders with tangible signs of disapproval. *Dörfer* was film director Wenders's initial attempt at directing a play, and he was faulted by critics for a literal reading of a nonliteral work. Moreover, what was the point, critics asked, of Handke's contemporary imitation of classical Greek theater? Handke, of course, was treading in the footsteps of other noted German-language practitioners of the closet drama – namely, Hölderlin and Hugo von Hofmannsthal. For example, Hofmannsthal, Richard Strauss's collaborator, had used Electra and Helen of Troy as subjects for opera and theater projects.

A 1981 interview with Krista Fleischmann and entries in his journal *Die Geschichte des Bleistifts* reveal that both *Kindergeschichte* and *Dörfer* were written at a time when Handke was preoccupied with the reading and analysis of Greek history and drama.[12] He told Fleischmann that Thucydides' history of the Peloponnesian War and its structuring of historical time was a model for his own treatment of time in *Kindergeschichte* (8). *Geschichte* reveals Handke's deep interest in Greek theater. There he analyzes the prototypical setting of Greek heroes ("their earth is a kingdom of light" [230]); the formulaic structure of their language ("a speech is often directed to a crowd with a reference to their village, i.e., as natives of that village" [231]); acting in Greek drama ("completely self-sufficient [*vollkommen selbstbewu*sst], even the murderers" [238]); and Aeschylus ("It seems he is the most capable and detailed of all trage-dians; no intrigue, only the power of words and pure drama" [237]). *Geschichte* also contains indirect references to Handke's working outline for *Dörfer*: the play would begin with fact, there would be no "rounded" characters, and the characters would strive to express a grand and archaic style of language. The journal also notes that the thematic resolution of *Dörfer* would mythologize art: "A goddess will appear and announce healing, in this way! 'It was never intended, that my race and yours should destroy themselves . . . !' Indeed, just as Thetis, coming from the depths of the earth and ocean, declares Peleus a god – just so must the language be at the end of my play; a spectacle of the gods" (*Geschichte*, 231).

Dörfer is thus an amalgam of classical literary texts centered on theory and Handke's understanding of Greek literary tradition. Handke also brings his brilliant scholarly facility with classical languages to his perceptive insight into classical history and litera-ture. As Klinkowitz and Knowlton assert, *Dörfer* signifies theatrically Handke's "return to the Greek stage in search of important models" (99); but the originality of *Dörfer* lies, too, in Handke's decision to incorporate distinct autobiographical elements into a classical con-text. The narrative of *Dörfer*, until the closing speech of the fourth scene, is derived from Handke's family history. Handke is the central character, Gregor, in *Dörfer*, but "Gregor" in his different aspects had appeared before as a major player in Handke's writing: as Gre-gor Keuschnig in *Stunde*, as Sorger in *Heimkehr*, and as the narrator-writer in *Sainte-Victoire*.

In the first scene of *Dörfer* Gregor is addressed by Nova, a female companion, as the "man from overseas," the "wanderer without a shadow," and the one who "failed to see the drops of blood in the snow" (*Dörfer*, 11). These are quotations, as it turns out, from various texts by Handke, Nietzsche, and Wolfram von Eschenbach, who wrote the medieval German epic *Parzival*. They help to establish Gregor's problematic and emblematic character for the reader at the beginning of the play. He is especially an outsider like Parzival, the young fool who in his search for the Holy Grail fails to see blood. Gregor, at the point of returning home after many years of living abroad, seeks counseling and direction from Nova, espe-cially for the resolution of the problems he will face in attempting to resolve a family crisis – namely, finding an answer to his brother Hans's letter. Hans had asked that Gregor mortgage the property that Gregor has inherited from their parents so that Sophie, their sister, could have money to open a shop. Gregor, however, has been estranged from his siblings for many years. He says: "I don't remember an instance of clear love for any one of them, but I do recall many moments of fear and anxiety" (*Dörfer*, 12). So his feelings about returning home are mixed, and he recalls his failure, as the family "intellectual" and spiritual "guide," to "rescue" both Hans and Sophie from the constriction of village life. (While in Alaska and elsewhere in North America, *Heimkehr*'s Sorger, a surrogate for Gregor, dreams of having abandoned his brother and sister.) Torn between his responsibility as the family head to make a right decision and the consequences of "betrayal" of his heritage should he decide to mortgage the property, Gregor has no clear insight into how he might resolve his problem. He says: "This place [his native village] is beautiful. It is more than trees and earth; it is a place of nurturing. . . . I cannot tolerate its becoming a place of sorrow" (*Dörfer*, 18).

Gregor decides to return to his home village, however, especially upon hearing the counsel of Nova, the semimythological guide and figure who urges him to "play the game, live dangerously. Don't play the leading character anymore. Be without a goal. Avoid doubts . . . be ready mentally to read signs. . . . Go across the villages" (*Dörfer*, 19-20). The intentionally obscure meaning behind Nova's speech is revealed only at the end of the play. Her words mystify the listener. They are an excellent sampling of Handke's way of reviving the rhetorical style of Greek classical theater and carrying out his wish, expressed in *Geschichte*, that his characters in *Dörfer* speak like prophets but not make prophecies (*Geschichte*, 236). "Take a chance," Nova tells Gregor "[at] another turn in the road and at another place" (*Dörfer*, 19). The first scene of *Dörfer* thus concludes with the introduction of the play's central motifs. This scene reveals the potential conflict in Gregor's possible refusal to go along with Hans and Sophie; it also brings forward Gregor's (and Handke's) feeling of longing for a sense of place, and his related fear that a familiar place will no longer exist. The symbolic sense of a familiar place is a continual theme in the *Heimkehr* tetralogy. As Doris Runzheimer points out in her analysis of *Dörfer*, it is for this reason, never entirely absent in the play, that Handke criticizes the devastation and trivialization of nature and village life by modern industry.[13] Runzheimer reads Sophie's plan to open a shop and live the life of a village entrepreneur as a concession to the march of commercialization. Under this reading, Gregor's decision to return to his village is essentially a move to secure the threatened peace of his village and "save a piece of heaven" from capitalist intervention. For the present, Gregor intends to reject any consideration of Sophie's plans. He fails, nevertheless, to see how these plans might function to give his sister a measure of self-control, identity, and independence.

The central conflict in the play between Gregor and his siblings seems to revolve around Gregor's definition of *Heimat* (home, birthplace) as a writer-artist and the evolution of a changing rural society, of which the village is an immediate example. Noting that Handke addresses this issue with intensity and personal reference in an entry in *Geschichte*, Renner asserts that these journal remarks are important inasmuch as they explain Gregor's (and Handke's) position in the first scene of the play, when Gregor is uncertain what to do for Sophie (*Dörfer*, 147). Handke asks, "What is tragic drama? That there is neither a people nor a homeland. Yet in the long run there is nothing else, only one's own homeland and one's people, if only to be loved as an idea. This is what I learned in years of living abroad" (*Geschichte*, 171). The subjective tone of these remarks transfers clearly into the narrative conflict of *Dörfer* itself.

The second scene of *Dörfer* introduces new characters and related themes and portrays the effects of industrialization in the village on the old and the young, on those dispossessed of land, and on the workers, who get the immediate economic benefit from the changing landscape of new jobs and the building projects that cover it. "In a dramatic poem," Handke notes in *Geschichte*, "the people should be foremost," and no one character should be "rounded" – that is, a fully developed figure (244-45). In the second scene Handke introduces the figure of the custodian, an old village woman obviously displaced and unhappy in her job as a watchman at the dormitories where Hans lives as a construction worker. She complains to Gregor of her alienation and disorientation in the village, the loss of familiar landmarks, and the invasion of city visitors and their experiments in country living. She asks rhetorically, "Where is the wilderness?" She prays for the arrival of the "unknown

Master of Industry . . . who will once again have the power to 'name' things" – that is, restore primeval nature (*Dörfer*, 26-27). Yet Gregor's brother Hans, whom he meets at the dormitory, seems to function well in the new environment. The brothers' meeting wavers between mutual acceptance and rejection. Critics of *Dörfer*'s theatrical premiere were puzzled by Hans's panegyric in the second scene on the "simple" life and by Hans and his fellow workers claiming membership in a "mysterious" community of workers and builders. For a time the language of Handke's play seems like a borrowing from Walt Whitman's *Leaves of Grass* and the American poet's well-known, melodramatic vision of America in the hands of the working class. Hans says to Gregor, "We are the fatherless ones, the free speakers, the homeless ones, those denied a sense of place, the beautiful strangers, men of all times" (*Dörfer*, 39).

Handke, an enemy of Brecht's working-class theater, finishes the second scene with workers' songs and chants that celebrate both the mystery and the alienation of a worker's life, closing with their wish that they be recognized by "a man of letters" and that they be allowed to share in the wealth of the world (*Dörfer*, 49). Gregor, however, believes that the mood of the workers reflects the misdirection and negativity behind the drive for modernity and industrialization. The workers' acceptance of the status quo is a mistake: it works against Gregor's expressed need to return home to the "place of his childhood" (*Dörfer*, 51).

Scene 3 presents a central point of conflict between Gregor and Sophie (whose name means "wisdom"). She begs her brother to allow the "realization" of her dream to open a shop: "Take your sister seriously and help her to achieve her own 'kingdom.' I have a right to it. The tiniest shop is a center for a friendly glow of light and – why not – someday for yourself" (*Dörfer*, 56). Gregor, however, feels that Sophie's plans would turn her into a caricature of a village woman wearing a "costume" and a "mask": "There will be a false melody in your voice, a false elegance in your body, from top to bottom a false energy. . . . Your 'sign' will be a rattling ring of key chains between your cold fingers" (*Dörfer*, 56-57).

Sophie's answer to Gregor's jeremiad against incipient commercialism, especially within his family circle, is vehement and convincing. She accuses him of not appreciating her need to become independent (Linstead 1988, 188). The conclusion of this brief scene (it is one of the shortest in the play) is tense, inconclusive, and potentially tragic in light of Gregor's underlying wish to stand as a redeemer in his village. Sophie's last word in this scene reminds him, however, that he "will become a 'helper' or nothing else. Everything you do will become unreal and I will become your 'dark sister'" (*Dörfer*, 60). A "dark sister" is naturally not a sister but a potential enemy, yet Sophie's wish for an alternative existence within the framework of modern village life is interesting and perhaps a valid alternative to dominance by the urban commercial principles seen by traditionalists like Gregor as a portent of the future. In this scene both Sophie and Gregor defend basically the same ideas, yet Gregor has thus far refused to support his sister's alternative point of view. His beliefs seem to be grounded in a view of nature as it existed before human intervention – that is, "the cliffs of yesteryear . . . parks and squares . . . the earth that man once called the kingdom of light" (*Dörfer*, 60).

The fourth scene, set within the village cemetery, begins with decidedly pessimistic speeches by Gregor, Hans, and Sophie. They make mutual accusations. His brother and sister expose the falsity of Gregor's role as a "savior" for the dying village. He is left with a dream rather than a practical, effective way to halt the destruction of his birthplace. In a moment of reverie he recalls the sound of ringing church bells from his youth: "Don't ever betray that sound. . . . Dramas are played out in places like this village. . . . Perhaps they are the last dramas. . . . The drama of dramas" (*Dörfer*, 67). His thoughts and words are, of course, only rhetorical bulwarks against what Handke, in another context, has called the "predetermined biography" of life – in this instance, the actual impoverishment of the village in its past history. The community is being abandoned by the poor villagers, who are eager to give up their heritage for material prosperity. So Gregor's dream of a "fast" rescue is naive and unworkable. He is reminded by an old inhabitant that the village is in "a land as small as it is mean, filled with prisoners, forgotten in their cells" (*Dörfer*, 74). At this point, deeply into a brown study, Gregor is confused and gives in to Hans's and Sophie's demands for money, not out of sympathy or compassion but out of despair: "Our kind has neither land nor property; we are only losers . . . rolling about our graves like pieces of cheese. . . . This is the last time we will see one another" (*Dörfer*, 85).

Handke's resolution of this crisis, arising from the irreconcilable differences between Gregor and his siblings on the one hand and the wider philosophical issue of saving the village on the other, is found in Nova's closing speech, a piece of dramatic rhetoric 11 pages long that makes a plea to all parties to heed the "healing" process of fantasy and vision as a means for "realization" of conflict. The end result, Nova infers, should be a higher level of existence. While there are no concrete proposals for change in Nova's speech – which functions here as a deus ex machina solution, taken from the devices of Greek tragedy – she also makes an appeal for love and for the power of illusion and vision in everyday life: "All participants in the conflict are invited to play the game, be of the Spirit. Each one of you is destined to be a World Conqueror" (*Dörfer*, 102). This speech, criticized by some readers and viewers as powerless to effect change within the context of today's world, is more than a facile borrowing from Nietzsche's *Zarathustra* or any similarly based inspirational text. To be fair to Handke, he has answered this criticism. As he stated in 1987, "Nova's speech is addressed first of all to artists and then to nonartists, reminding both of Art as a mediator of conflict. . . . The speech was also my response to the general tone of negativity with which I seemed to be ending the poem. . . . I wanted another kind of 'music' to be heard."[14]

Thus what seems at first to be an unworkable solution to the personal and social conflicts of the play is actually an appeal by Handke to our deepest utopian instincts; art and artists, he proposes, can point the way toward viable, transcendent, and abstract solutions to political and economic problems. Gregor, as a symbol in the play of the artist-reformer Handke, is instructed by Nova to "go through the villages" to broadcast and implement her art, a "new comprehension of peace, beauty, nature and art that can serve as an impetus to transformation for others" (Klinkowitz and Knowlton, 103). In *Dörfer* Handke seems to accept his role as a standard-bearer for art and esthetics, which function as vehicles for the renewal of social processes and the elimination of social discord.

Chapter Six

New Prose: Meditative Fiction

Andreas Loser, the symbolic narrator-protagonist of Handke's 1983 novel *Der Chinese des Schmerzes* (Across) is a brooding, meditative teacher of classical languages at a school in the suburbs of Salzburg.[1] Loser, as his name connotes in English translation, is an outsider and loner, a type familiar to readers of *Angst* and *Stunde*. Loser is also an amateur archeologist who spends his spare time uncovering historical and cultural artifacts. His specialty is finding thresholds of houses, churches, and temples in the vicinity of the city. He writes an occasional scholarly article on his researches for the *Salzburg Yearbook for Regional Studies*. Early in the text Loser explains that his passion for archeology and his unique approach to the study of ancient thresholds are a consequence of an observation once made to him by an older archeologist. This man told Loser that he only "wanted to find something, so that during our digs, I tried more to avoid what was there than what was not, no matter how it had 'gone away.' What was missing was in fact still there, either in 'space' or as an 'empty form.' In this way, I acquired skill in finding [thresholds], which are missed by trained archeologists" (*Chinese*, 24).

Handke's novel, 255 pages in its German edition, consists of three parts and a brief epilogue. Each part furthers the account of Loser's spiritual and philosophical development as a "crosser of thresholds" and a storyteller, "threshold" signifying a moving over, a transition point, a rite of passage from personal isolation to social integration. Loser is his own narrator in the novel and is referred to by Handke as the "viewer" in each part title; he is initially depicted as a man in a state of existential suspension, a symbol of a contemporary Everyman whose fate has parabolic significance and narrative interest. As Renner states, "The story that Loser tells is not only his own, but is about the act of narration, too" (161).[2] Loser's storytelling in *Chinese* is thus intended by Handke as a confession of a life as well as a way in which it can be told.

In the first part of the novel "Der Betrachter wird abgelenkt" (The Viewer is diverted), Loser is living alone in a functional suburban apartment, separated by choice from his wife and children. He is on a voluntary leave of absence from his teaching duties and spends a good amount of daylight time looking down onto the panorama of the landscape. Nature and objects interest him, and his nighttime reading of Virgil's *Georgics* gives his "viewing" a purpose, focusing as it does on elements of nature. Virgil's words and sentences bring Loser down to earth, into the realm of animals, horticulture, and the concrete details of life, those connections that Loser feels he has lost. Loser values Virgil's account of the ancient world not only for the "living" adjectives that grace the poet's nouns but also because he offers an accessible entry into another "story": the one-on-one identity of the writing of poetry with things themselves. But Loser is also a connoisseur of privation; always aware of rifts and absences, he is a man who understands the fine distinction between "emptiness" and "being empty," the latter being an "empty form." In this sense, "being empty" affords Loser esthetic and spiritual possibilities: direct awareness of nature; insight into the naïveté of nature; and the recovery of a pastoral world in which civilization and nature are one internal experience (the classical dream of Arcadia). Hence Loser's intense preoccupation with excavating and internalizing the threshold experience.

Handke points out, however, that Loser's present reclusiveness began as a consequence of conflict between himself and the external world. As Loser recalls: "One afternoon in the *Getreidegasse*, less crowded than usual, a man overtook and ran into me. He turned toward a display window, and we both ran into one another. The truth is, this wasn't a 'real' collision, since I could have stepped aside. I had given him a shove intentionally" (*Chinese*, 19).

Loser discovers within himself a facility for violence. This incident, however, occurring as it does on a not-so-busy street in Salzburg, is an *acte gratuit*, a gratuitous or inconsequential action performed on impulse, possibly to gratify a desire for sensation. It is the first of two such actions – the second happens in part 2 – that lead to Loser's insight that he is a "repository" of patent facts and unanswered questions. Loser is overcome by depression

(*Schwermut*) over the incident in downtown Salzburg. He knows that his treatment of the stranger is morally suspect, and at the very least that he is someone vulnerable to becoming indiscriminately violent. Like André Gide's young antihero Lafcadio in the novel *Les Caves des Vatican* (1924), Loser is willing to confront the fact of his impulsive action, but unlike Lafcadio, Loser moves at first into a state of moral and ethical indecision over the consequences of his act. He is not rendered entirely immobile by his action, however, and he ascribes his passivity to a state of "having time," which he construes as a "state of grace." In crossing this specific threshold Loser is neither guilty nor innocent, and Handke defers final judgment in this affair since Loser is destined to undergo another threshold crossing.

The second incident occurs in part 2, "Der Betrachter greift ein" (The Viewer takes action), during his walk to a monthly card game at the home of a friend on the Mönchsberg, mountains in the Salzburg environs. Loser picks up a stone and kills an old man who is busy painting a swastika on the trunks of birch trees. Loser's discovery of the swastika had made him furious. The painted swastika for Loser symbolizes more than the survival of marginal politics, and certainly more than a prankster's desecrating of the forest. Loser reflects that the swastika defines not only his special melancholy but all melancholy and artificialty in Austria (*Chinese*, 97). He must make a fast decision – another threshold crossing – and in doing so, he takes deadly aim at the head of the swastika painter. Handke, however, asks his reader to suspend credibility that Loser has committed murder, since Loser escapes an encounter with the law over the civil consequences of his act. While Handke does not ignore the legal or moral implications of what has transpired, he seems more interested in pointing out that the murder is carried out with a stone, not a gun or a knife. The episode, in fact, is an occasion for a visionary passage in which Handke transforms the setting of the murder (a forested, secluded area in the mountain) into a romantically inspired fantasy. For a moment, the killing is suspended between reality and esthetic feeling. Loser feels like an outcast, yet he is "transformed," a witness to the world's power and beauty. Strong wind on the mountain ushers in the "groaning" appearance of a "swan" flying above Loser and his victim. The scene is both magnificent and ambiguous (*Chinese*, 104). The murder of the swastika painter is placed by Handke in the context of spiritual and esthetic regeneration and thus becomes, through the image of the white swan, a positive sign, a symbol for Loser's growth and change. Handke intends for the murder and its aftermath to function as a process of catharsis and regeneration. In this second key incident of the text Handke stresses the existentialist import of Loser's act. In a 1987 interview with Herbert Gamper, Handke noted that Loser's fury at the discovery of the swastika is not only anger at the continuous presence of past history in his homeland; for Loser the swastika is also a symbol of his personal depression (22). He has no other choice, he believes, but to kill the perpetrator. Loser finally throws the body over the mountain cliff, and for a moment, perhaps as a sign of "higher" justice, he is pulled downward with the falling body.

From this point on Loser is intensely preoccupied with the reconstruction of his life, an endeavor that requires both acknowledgment to himself that he is a murderer and the devising of a unique a plan to reenter the world. He resolves to become a "listener" and attends carefully in part 2 to the wide-ranging explanations offered by his fellow cardplayers when, at the end of their game, the group is drawn by Loser into a discussion of "thresholds." Loser is especially interested in the response of one cardplayer, a priest from whom he expects a moral and ethical exegesis on the pitfalls of crossing over onto the "wrong side." The priest says no such thing, only noting that though religious tradition has little to say about thresholds as material objects, it does reflect on them as the symbolic passage from one "zone" to another. Thresholds, says the priest, exist in a state between waking and dreaming. Every threshold is both an instance of and an opportunity to achieve threshold consciousness. Finally, thresholds are a resource of inner powers for those who cross them. This episode is one of the most original and brilliant parts of the novel. Handke suggests that the priest's ideas on thresholds are not entirely the author's own thoughts; the priest refers to the ideas of an unnamed "modern teacher," perhaps Heidegger (*Chinese*, 67).

Themes of rebirth and renewal are predominant in the third part, "Der Betrachter sucht einen Zeuger" (The Viewer seeks a witness). The epilogue's closing image of Loser is no longer the mournful one of the "suffering Chinaman" alluded to several times in the text, and in the German title of the novel; now he is a contemplative and joyful man, standing on a bridge near his apartment, an observant figure watching the ebb and flow of daily life in Salzburg. The canal, the light, the willows will all "survive." This final scene signifies both a spiritual and secular acceptance by Loser of the "real" world, however mundane or trivial it might be. Submission to the unnamed "giver," however, is not achieved by Loser without struggle or cost, for at the beginning of the third part Loser is still depicted as a man living within the trauma of an experiential process. A crossing of thresholds has heightened Loser's receptivity to change and metamorphosis, a process providing him insight that whatever was deadly or life-inhibiting within himself could be overcome.

Loser has lived between depression and cheerfulness. Reflecting that throwing a stone at the swastika painter marked the beginning of his own "death," Loser, like Faust before his attempt at suicide, was plunged into another depression, fearful of dying without love or human contact (a witness). In an episode in part 3 reminiscent of Faust's rebirth on Easter day, Loser is inspired by the sounds of ringing church bells inviting the citizens of Salzburg to celebrate the Easter feast. Loser is impelled to make a physical journey of renewal that includes visits to people and places bound to the shards of his former life. This journey not only bears witness to a previously unfulfilled life; it is also a seeking of witnesses – that is, a search for people who will listen to his story, the parts of which Loser is careful to recall in the right order. Loser, whose story is finally a meditative threshold story, and whose identity as a human being merges into that of a parabolic storyteller, begins to retrace his steps at the city airport, which is revealed as a barren place except for Loser's unplanned sexual encounter. He visits his senile mother, an encounter that forces him to reassess their relationship. He makes an ex tempore flight to Italy and visits Virgil's birthplace in Mantua; there he searches for the geographical sources of places mentioned in *Georgics*. He returns eventually to his teaching career. His principal cites Loser's eccentricity and deviation from the norm as the reasons for his popularity with students. Most important, Loser visits his wife and children, but he moves among them only as a familiar face and a tolerated occasional visitor. He wins anew the respect of his son, who, when he hears his father's story, is incredulous. The son relates to the meaning of his father's rebellion: the redefinition of personal values and the rebirth of identity. Both Loser and his family are comfortable with this confession that portends hope and redirection. The final image of Loser in the epilogue, standing on a bridge, is thus an apt symbol to close with inasmuch as it portrays the dual functions of Loser as a doer and an observer. Doing and observing have coalesced at a transition point, at a threshold, strongly denoting that Loser might move in one of two directions; but he has learned to stop and reflect, to gather himself.

Chinese is clearly a novel that challenges conventional morality and ethics through its implied defense of heightened experience, but the finality of such a judgment is obviated through Handke's convincing portrait of a man in spiritual and existential crisis; or, as Renner has noted, the reader is confronted with the "apotheosis of the storyteller," who, as it turns out, is equally the center of philosophical probity in the novel (172).

Die Wiederholung

Handke continues his self-revelation in *Die Wiederholung* (Repetition), a 1986 text that expands the autobiographical themes first adumbrated in *Brief, Unglück*, and the *Heimkehr* tetralogy.[3] These earlier works contain relevant details about the writer's birthplace in Altenmarkt, the painful and agonizing trauma of economic privation, and, finally, the lingering specter of recent Austrian political history. Within this context of the unresolved cultural and social problems Handke is now integrating into the narrative structures of his recent fiction stands the question of ethnic identity. As an Austrian citizen of Slovene ancestry, Handke treats cultural issues related to home, family, and language. In *Wiederholdung* Filip Kobal (the author's mask), now a much older man, tells of a 1960 trip to Jesenice, a neighboring Slovene city, to search for his missing brother, Gregor. His classmates had set out for Greece, but Gregor went off to Yugoslavia by himself. Since he came from a bilingual area of southern Carinthia, he felt he had an excuse to cross the border.

Filip was searching for clues about his lost brother, but the facts about his brother's disappearance were scarce. There were only the family's memories, encompassing both reality and fiction, in which the truth was hidden by an adoring mother and a dour father in his role as a cruel paterfamilias. Gregor, about 20 years older than Filip, was once an agricultural student in Maribor, the capital city of neighboring Slovenia, the Yugoslavian republic south of Austrian

Carinthia. Slovenia, with its own language and distinct culture, is regarded as the ancestral and linguistic home of those Austrians "confined" to Carinthia under the exigencies of twentieth-century European history. Slovenia and Carinthia once shared a common destiny under the hegemony of the Austrian-Hungarian empire. We learn that at the beginning of World War II Gregor was inducted into the Austrian army but went AWOL, probably to join a group of antifascist partisans. Filip, after graduating from a *Gymnasium* in Klagenfurt, decides only later to search for his missing brother, a quest that begins with little more than Gregor's student copybook containing notes on horticulture and a Slovene-German dictionary. A genealogical and linguistic trek into the interior of neighboring Slovenia develops into a leading motif of Handke's book. *Wiederholung* emulates the framework of a bildungsroman, if only for its obvious borrowing of the prototypical protagonist's journey into a wider world. In *Wiederholung* this is a journey into the meaning and pattern of ethnicity, Gregor's family history, and the art of living itself.[4] Feelings, thoughts, and memory – 25 years have passed for the middle-aged narrator of *Wiederholung* – are the devices through which Handke develops the narrative. The style of the narrative is rhapsodic and epiphanal, secular and religious, singular and simultaneous in the expression of emotions and feelings, and never straightforward chronologically. For Filip, however, the quality of memory becomes most important, remembering being a more exacting activity than random thinking. Memory, he notes, is "work" and as such situates experience in a definite sequence. It is because of memory that Filip the older man can tell the story of his search.

In the first part, "Das blinde Fenster" (The Blind window), the narrator as a young man crosses the border between his country and Yugoslavia. The journey brings to mind the extended memory of local schools, the village of Rinkenberg, conditions in his father's home, and his estranged feeling that he was not what he "purported to be," that he was "only pretending" to be a viable part of village and family life. Part 1 sets the background and explains why Filip Kobal is the author's ideal figure to begin this special journey into the linguistic and cultural elements of his ethnic past. The narrator reveals that his mother was a woman whom he remembers as a busy, running figure in the kitchen, where she showed her skills as a housewife; but she daringly intervened to save him from the tyranny

of classmates and teachers at the *Gymnasium* as well as at the seminary. Handke includes an autobiographical episode in *Wiederholung*, told through his narrator. Filip recalls an especially mean
encounter with a seminary teacher (without religious orders) who
tried to define his young student and protect him from the mark of
academic mediocrity: "I was driven to break the picture [*das Bild*]
he had conceived of myself. I wanted to retreat, as I had hidden for
sixteen years" (*Wiederholung*, 36).

Filip, gradually becoming an outsider in the village, haunts the
streets and places where he can revel in his anonymity, longing for
contact with buses, trains, and stations. His restlessness is reflected
in, if not supported by, the discovery that his parents, like himself,
were village "strangers." This is a judgment, however, that the parents have made of themselves. Filip recalls the aberrant behavior of
these self-styled exiles, with their brooding and fits of melancholia,
as the result of a combination of factors – chiefly, those events surrounding the execution of a rebel Slovenian ancestor, the emigration
of others into Austria, and the effect of this episode on Filip's father.
His father was obsessed by the execution and the forced emigration,
which accounted for the family's poverty, unemployment, and
homelessness. Filip's mother, taking her cue from her husband's
indignities over the course of his life in the Austrian village of
Rinkenberg, lives with the dream that her two sons might reclaim
"their place" in the southwest, over the border, though Filip notes
that she never made a trip to Yugoslavia. Place names and ethnic
conflicts over the years become lyrically and mythically embellished
in young Filip's imagination. He admits that the essence of modern
Slovenia lies somewhere between his parents' stories and those several letters from his brother in the years between the wars. Filip
faults his father's inability to live peacefully and harmoniously with
himself and his family; this is an additional reason for Filip to search
for a solution to the riddle of his marginal life at home and in the
village. At best, Filip can only dream of a family reunion in the dark,
Rinkenberg living room, with his brother reappearing in tears but
thankful for his family's lingering affection. This dream seems to be
the prime reason behind young Filip's decision to cross the Austrian
border and begin his odyssey into the Slovene interior, a trip that is
as yet neither defined nor clearly explicated. He finds inspiration,
however, in a "blind window" set in a wall of the local train station,

from which he departs for his short journey over the frontier. The window not only reminds him of the lost eye suffered by Gregor during a failed bout with ophthalmic fever but seems to him a portent of other "blind windows" that will accompany him as "objects of research" and "signposts" in the recovery of his past.

The full meaning of the second part's title, "Die leeren Viehsteige" (The Empty cow paths), is revealed only at its end. In Jesenice, Filip finds the Slovene world awash with details of life presented to him as signs joining to form legible writing (*Wiederholung*, 114). If this is Handke's language to indicate that Filip, like the author, is preoccupied with the perception of signs and names, then Filip's first hours are a deciphering, a "reading" of cultural differences between life in Austria and Yugoslavia. He feels that he has lived for almost 20 years in a country without a definite identity. On the other hand, Yugoslavia did not claim him for compulsory schooling or military draft. This was the land of his ancestors, and he therefore embraces it freely. Filip feels free because he is finally "stateless" (*Wiederholung*, 119).

Filip's first morning in Jesenice is suffused not only with the rosy glow of youthful, impulsive sensation but with a feeling of liberation, which he ascribes to an unbelabored experience of congruence, to the simultaneity of two activities that are each voluntarily offered and accepted. Serendipity characterizes congruence, Filip notes, along with an absence of appraisal and judgment by the cultural majority. People on the street in Jesenice are, like Filip himself, "kingless and stateless," members of a race of journeymen and hired hands. Pedestrians and objects suit one another. He breathes anew. He gets a second wind, an ability to "read" a Slovene newspaper whose headlines, he notices, are pure news, the opposite of his German-language newspaper back home. And he even understands the conversation of people around him (*Wiederholung*, 132).

Filip is thus not tempted to return to Austria on the morning train. Instead he buys a ticket to the southwest, the Bohinj region of legend and the subject of his mother's prayers. There he goes to a hamlet named, appropriately, Pozabljeno ("the forgotten place," or "the place of forgetfulness"). His being left alone is natural and of little consequence. He has his privacy.

Filip begins the job of reading and deciphering Gregor's copybook and German-Slovene dictionary. In translating Slovene words from Gregor's copybook, Filip moves from "blind reading" to "sighted reading," a transference first into imagery and then into words, especially when Gregor's way of explaining a simple matter leads him to imagine a tale out of fiction, a story of a hero's attachment to a place. The memory of his brother's "airy radiance" as opposed to his mother's "heaviness" reveals Filip's adulation and near worship of his brother. Filip's discovery of the Slovene dictionary becomes an icon of his Bohinj stay and contributes to his understanding of the people and culture of that region, especially in their specificity and ahistoricity – timeless, yet living in seasonal time. Filip finds that the Slovene language has only a few borrowed words for war and authority, whereas his native German has many. Slovene excels, too, in the construction of diminutives. The Slovene dictionary is a portal into Filip's memory of village life in Rinkenberg. Words in the dictionary communicate images of the long-forgotten childhood landscape: animals, food, grass, and trees. These words also give Filip "images of the world" for which actual experience is not a necessity. A world takes shape around any random word from the dictionary, such as a chestnut husk, or even the words for tobacco left in a pipe. Other words create circles and images from ancient times – that is, the era of Orpheus.

Wiederholung suggests that, for Filip, Gregor's copybook, especially his dictionary, is an illuminating text allied to a special law of writing, evoking the breath of life. Specific words from the language of the Slovenes are signs or emblems of universal experience. Slovene words (Gregor's words) free Filip from melancholy and depression. They are therapeutic. The dictionary teaches Filip that there is a word for everything and every situation. The copybook is likewise an educational device, containing the notes of a man about to embark on a project similar to Filip's: research, reflection and meditation. The copybook, Filip notes early on, resembles a bildungsroman in instructing the reader on the cultivation and husbandry of apple trees. Gregor's metaphors and allusions to human growth in the care of fruit trees actually relate to stages of the human condition. The story of a particular fruit orchard (described in Gregor's copybook) is in fact Gregor's in Rinkenberg, and it reveals Gregor as Filip's doppelgänger in seeking wisdom for the meaning and pattern of life.

In the Bohinj, the dictionary as a revelatory text mystically directs Filip's eyes toward the southern chain of mountains and an adjacent slope of pasture laced with "empty cow paths." These cow paths, so integral a part of the regional rural landscape, inspire Handke to meditate on the symbolism of emptiness and annihilation, the image of a migration of unnamed people and animals reaching back to the origins of time. Now the cow paths lead to nowhere. As "stairs" they remain unused. Young Filip mourns and grieves, and he "reads" the paths as a metaphor linked to his missing brother, whose disappearance symbolizes the absence of all those who can no longer speak or even write with words.

In the last part of the novel, "Die Savanna der Freiheit und das neunte Land" (The Savannah of freedom and the ninth country), Filip is in the final stage of his genealogical and linguistic journey. This is played out in the coastland area of the Karst, a Slovene landscape that is physically and geographically similar to Gregor and Filip's native village. The Karst is an archaic region. Its utilitarian simplicity is reflected in the style of its people and the architecture of their dwellings. Household furniture and implements teach Filip the heritage of his ancestors. The most outstanding image (and discovery) for Filip in the Karst, however, occurs in the context of a metaphorical vision. Believing himself lost in the wilderness, Filip arrives at the edge of a *dolina*, a deep recession in the earth. This bowl-shaped hole is lined with terraces covered with small fields and gardens being worked by an entire population. Their work is slow and graceful; the sound of a hoe working the ground characterizes and defines the Karst (*Wiederholung*, 287).

For Filip, this image is sensual to the point of rapture, a vision simultaneously of continuity and renewal on the one hand and a goal to strive for on the other. Filip comes to the point when he must admit that his motives for coming to Slovenia and the Karst were many, among them, to fulfill the gaps in his ancestral memory and earn the respect of his forebears. The meaning of Gregor's passage through Slovenia becomes clearer to Filip. Here Handke shifts thematic direction on the unsuspecting reader, who, still concerned that Filip's trip into the Slovenian interior may uncover traces of the missing brother, will have failed to notice that Filip has found the true object of his quest. He perceives that the best way to preserve his brother's memory is not to "find" him but to tell a story about him.[5] Filip will become a writer, a creator of word images. And the meaning of one of Gregor's last letters to his family, sent from the World War II front, is also clarified – namely, that access to the Ninth Country, the legendary country of Slovenia and the collective ancestral goal of the Kobal family in Austria, can be gained through writing and through storytelling. Filip has found his vocation: he will be a storyteller. "Story," says the middle-aged narrator at the end of the novel, "[is] the most spacious of all vehicles and heavenly chariots. Eye of my story, become my reflection" (*Wiederholung*, 333). Filip prays as an adoring worshiper before the statue of the storyteller's muse. Had Filip chosen not to search for Gregor, the art of storytelling would never have changed the course of his life. Filip never finds Gregor in the Karst or in the whole of Slovenia. Only the letters of his name survive, carved into the face of a school chapel, a not insignificant reminder that Gregor, too, "passed" through the city of Maribor on a journey of self-discovery and revelation.

Nachmittag eines Schriftstellers

Both the title and content of Handke's 1987 novella *Nachmittag eines Schriftstellers* (The Afternoon of a writer) allude to the American short story "Afternoon of an Author," written by F. Scott Fitzgerald in 1936.[6] "Author" is a fictional account of a day in Fitzgerald's creative life, from morning to early evening. Arthur Mizener says that "Author" is a late work and that Fitzgerald makes the "tension of his feelings" the central focus of the reader's interest (Mizener, 11). These tensions, it turns out, are strikingly similar to those of the writer-protagonist in Handke's book, a text actually dedicated to Fitzgerald. A key question in both texts is, How does a writer achieve sustenance and balance in the slippery relationship between life and art? For Fitzgerald, there is a writer's ironic but " unquestioned acceptance of what he and his world are and an acute awareness of what they might be and, indeed, in some respects at least once were" (Mizener, 10). Handke's unnamed writer (probably Handke himself) is a European living in an unidentified European city that resembles Salzburg. Fitzgerald's setting is Baltimore, near the campus of Johns Hopkins University. Both Fitzgerald's story and Handke's novella track a complicated set of feelings and perceptions that mark the creative paths of their protagonists. Right at the start, both Handke's and Fitzgerald's writers are confronted with a dilemma that reflects upon their future ability to continue writing. For Fitzgerald's protagonist, "the problem was a magazine story that had become so thin in the middle that it was about to blow away. The plot was like climbing endless stairs, he had no element of surprise in reserve, and the characters who started so bravely day-before-yesterday couldn't have qualified for a newspaper serial" (Mizener, 178). And for Handke's: "Didn't the problem found in his craft parallel that of his existence, that he could not be consistent and disciplined? That is, a problem not of 'I' as a writer but rather, 'the writer as I' " (*Nachmittag*, 5-6).

The two writers both stop working in early afternoon. Handke's protagonist declares that the day's work has gone well; he can thus leave his house with a safe professional conscience. He hopes that a walk will open up his senses to sounds and sights, in short, bring about a restoration of the business of living. Fitzgerald's author tears up everything he has written after "redlining good phrases in red crayon" (Mizener, 178) – there will be, he declares, no more writing today. Both men have a plan for their outing, and as Handke and Fitzgerald point out, that plan seems to validate an escape into the outside world, the realm of life beyond the seclusion of the writer's study. Handke's writer will walk down a stairway into the city, then return to the suburbs. Fitzgerald's character simply boards a city bus, from which there is much to see: a football field, pedestrian traffic, the entrance into downtown Baltimore. He will go to a hotel barbershop, and to that end he leaves home with a bottle of shampoo ointment in his hand.

A primary question for Handke, however, is whether his writer will gain anything from this decision to establish contact with life, whether it be crossing a bridge, eating a meal in a restaurant, or reading a postcard from a "lost" friend in America. He tries to overcome his basic fear that writing and the writer are anachronistic relics of twentieth-century culture. Observation and intuition emerge in Handke's text as the strongest tools of the writer's vocation, and they are conveyed in several detailed encounters that the writer has with the "real" world, actual or imagined, fateful meetings between the creative personality and its fragile vision of the "other" environment. This vision, though eccentric, is shown to be relevant to the writer's solitary life. Connections between life and art are made. For example, the squares of the unnamed European city, which

Handke's writer is shown entering from the back, are a metaphor for the structural features of his writing. The texture and the composition of the squares are what intrigues him; he sees what the average viewer cannot discern. Their parts mirror the elements of his prose. Once he perceives this correspondence, however, he starts to run: "Even though the square [he had just crossed] was near the river and in the lowest area of the city, he made a diagonal as though it was a high plateau" (*Nachmittag*, 28). Reading a city paper, with the jealousy and feuding between critics and writers on its arts pages, is disorienting and depressing. Though the writer has now retreated from open controversy, relying on his own strength, the newspaper brings back the memory of his apprentice years as a younger writer.

Handke next sets his writer down on a crowded downtown street, in the midst of Christmas shoppers. The bends and turns of this street (*Trossgasse*) move along with the stream of perceptions that flows into the mind of the writer-protagonist. The street is not a guarantor of anonymity, and he tries to avoid recognition; yet he looks into bookstore windows to spot his books. He feels assaulted by stares from the public, since he embodies what it hates: dreams, writing, disagreement, and, finally, art. He is cornered into giving a stranger an autograph, an act he resents because it compels him to play the part of a writer. Any similar episode denoting confrontation or antagonism between the writer and his public is missing from Fitzgerald's story, which conveys only a hint that the author questions the earlier adulation of the critics about his writing, who said that his artistic viability was "indefatigable" and therefore his writing career seemed full of promise (Mizener, 181). In fact, Fitzgerald's protagonist, in contrast to Handke's, avoids bitterness when he reflects on the real state of his affairs. The reader's walk with Handke's writer, on the other hand, seems like a stroll with a misanthropic bachelor who is ready for a confrontation over any imagined slight. Given the opportunity to begin again, there would be no more photographs, or even autographs, for the adoring public.

As an examination of the processes of artistic creativity, *Nachmittag* reveals that both the artist and the nonartist depend on experience, that both use experience as a primary point of departure. For the artist, however, experience is then transformed into the stuff of art, which is abetted by observation, intuition, and the related necessities of "namelessness" and "isolation" (*Nachmittag*, 49). A key

comment in Handke's text is that loneliness and anonymity are catalysts to creativity (*Nachmittag*, 55). Nameless "things" can be
reduced (as they often are) to bare objects and a sense of emptiness,
even after the writer's experience in the real world. Emptiness
teaches the writer-artist that it is a source of inner richness and
esthetic plenitude, the wellspring of true creative renewal. (Handke
espouses similar ideas about the origins of artistic inspiration in
Chinese.)

Nachmittag includes a telling episode set in a suburban bar. The
writer decides to go there before he retires for the night. A drunk,
suspecting that the writer is scarcely listening to him and that the
writer is a "fraudulent" outsider in this environment, is almost successful in making the writer question his "business" – that is, he
nearly gains an admission from the writer that he is a failure in the
social community. The drunk calls him a liar and a weakling, words
with which the writer seems to agree, for they appear to be true. This
is a splendid opportunity for the writer to pity his abused and misunderstood state and to relish his morbidity. This incident is echoed
in another key dialogue of the text, one between the writer and his
translator, an elderly man who has come to the city to confer on a
problem of translation. In a peculiar turn of events, the translator
seizes the occasion to confess that, in years gone by, he had the wisdom to abandon plans to become a writer. Unlike a writer, he notes,
a translator "knows he will be needed by society. Therefore I have
lost any anxiety. . . . I have become relaxed in a superficial way.
When I cover up your 'wound' as well as I can, I'm also hiding my
own" (*Nachmittag*, 81-82). Handke's writer not only understands
but assimilates the messages behind the translator's speech.

After returning home, the writer wonders whether the experiences of his enervating walk were reality or hallucination. He feels as
if he has been engaged in a personal battle with the outside world,
yet he goes to bed intending to reclaim himself for the next day: "I
began as a narrator. Endure. Let things be. Let them matter. Transmit. Let me be the craftsman of the most sensitive materials"
(*Nachmittag*, 90-91). These affirming words answer those unsettling
doubts that earlier challenged the stability of the writer's vocation:
he accepts his original decision to be a writer; he agrees to let the
outside world go about its business; he has his place and a role in
society. He manages to connect his art to his life. Fitzgerald's writer,

on the other hand, returns home from his excursion with a lesser sense of artistic and cultural mission. Fitzgerald says of him, "He needed reforestation and he was well aware of it, and he hoped the soil would stand one more growth. It had never been the very best soil for he had an early weakness for showing off instead of listening and observing . . . he was quite tired – he would lie down for ten minutes and see if he could get started on an idea in the two hours before dinner" (Mizener, 182).

Confrontation, bitterness, and paranoia can be the writer's fate, but they are burdens that Handke's writer accepts in his persona as a hermetic, obsessed creature. For a solitary craftsman, there exists a singular reward. This reward, however, is centered on the answers found to those mysteries generated in a writer's study whenever he begins to write. "Readership, a public, and public attention seem violations, embarrassments, beside the point," noted John Updike when he reviewed Handke's novella. Aptly commenting on its implications for the writer's craft, he added, "The Mysteries the writer nurtures in his or her study are beyond explaining. . . . The writer's artifacts are like shoes that disdain actual feet."[7]

Die Abwesenheit

The short text *Die Abwesenheit* (1987; Absence) is subtitled "A Fairy Tale," the only one of Handke's prose writings with this distinction.[8] Thematically, *Abwesenheit* is a meditative, philosophical tale that offers an Eastern solution to Western problems of aberration and social estrangement. In this sense, *Abwesenheit* is linked to Handke's other texts that focus on contemporary isolation and separation. Generically, *Abwesenheit* brings to mind the fairy-tale collections of the Brothers Grimm and related tales (*Kunstmärchen*) written by Ludwig Tieck, E. T. A. Hoffmann, and Clemens Brentano, German romantics of the early nineteenth century. In its standard form, the German fairy tale contains experiences bordering on the supernatural and motifs of magic, metamorphosis, and witchcraft. They usually have a happy ending in which virtue is rewarded and evil punished. The primary setting of Handke's modern fairy tale is an unnamed European city from which four characters make a common journey to a desertlike plateau, "an oval reaching out to the horizon . . . its own kingdom, separated from reality, not a mere landscape, but a unique country, a continent above our continent" (*Abwesenheit*,

121). Journeys, dreams, and wanderings through paradisiacal landscapes are other common characteristics of the German fairy tale, yet these same devices have also been assimilated into Eastern fairy tales in which such traveling is often synonymous with inner development or spiritual roaming. The Eastern traveler becomes an adept, a potential disciple, and is accompanied through a higher world by a practitioner of mythic realization. The magician figure of the German (i.e., the Western) fairy tale thus becomes the wordless sage in the Eastern one. At the conclusion of their common adventures, the Eastern sage may abandon his disciple, leaving little trace of himself behind. Their journey finished, the sage intentionally dissolves the pupil-teacher relationship.

One can only speculate on the literary sources of *Abwesenheit*, but the text is preceded and concluded by two short excerpts from the writing of the Chinese Taoist master Chuang-tzu, from the fourth century B.C. His work is a sophisticated yet practical commentary on Lao-tzu, the patriarch of Taoism whose teachings (unlike Chuang-tzu's) focused on the role of the Tao (the Way) in civil government. The singular message of the first excerpt relates to the central theme of Handke's book: "A horse of the kingdom – his qualities are complete. Now he looks anxious, now to be forgetting himself. Such a horse prances along, or pushes on spurning the dust and now knowing where he is."[9]

This short parable says much about Taoism. According to Chuang-tzu, the "perfect horse" is the "perfect Taoist," who is attuned to the Way and moves with the "imperceptible" and the "indiscernible," accepting both the invisibility and the latent particularity of the Way. *Abwesenheit* proposes at the very least a similar religious or philosophical thought – namely, that man must learn to interact with the universe, which, in turn, contains a society functioning within a cyclical movement of time, rhythm, and the law of return. These fundamental Eastern (Taoist) concepts define the structure and meaning of Handke's book. All four parts demonstrate, in this sense, wider aspects of Eastern religious teachings; it is possible, however, to read Handke's text within Taoist terms alone.

The four characters in *Abwesenheit* are generic figures who typify segments of twentieth-century social and cultural alienation: an old man, a young woman, a soldier, and a gambler. The old man views the outside world with indifference; he lives in a sanatorium for the elderly. He is literally an observer and recorder of exterior activity: he spends days looking out the window of his room and encoding images, using mysterious symbols and signs, in a book. The young woman is also engaged in writing a book. She is imagined by the reader as defiant and despairing, a combatant, perhaps, for self-identity. Her lover has called her a bundle of contradictions and claims that she has no response to anything other than themselves, that she is unresponsive to work, nature, or history. He has accused her of being obsessed with love and thus failing to see that even lovers need something other than themselves. Introduced next in the first chapter of the text is the soldier, an unhappy man who is clearly in the wrong profession. In the text he is the subject of a stinging, vindictive attack by his mother who, on the point of his returning to duty, says that she had always hoped for a "different" son, a different person: "Instead of becoming someone else, you're more removed than you ever were. After all this time in the service, you haven't got any award. You have never claimed your 'place,' either in the military or anywhere. Your comrades treat you as though you were only air. Nobody looks at you" (*Abwesenheit*, 30-31). Finally, the gambler is introduced. He may be an "artist" at gambling, but he is so dependent on being "alert" that he is never, paradoxically, anywhere. He longs to begin a new life, to feel and grieve the loss of love, to know true danger.

These strangers will board a common train in the middle of the city. What they share is a sense of deeply felt exclusion in an interventionist society. Their community functions beyond the pale of the Taoist ideal, the ideal of the unselfconscious symbiosis of a society attuned to the cycles and rhythms of nature. Handke's characters in *Abwesenheit* choose to flee their society rather than remain; they opt for the life of the adept and the spiritual adventure into the unknown. They choose to renounce contrivances set up by their society for acceptance and recognition. The young girl gives up a lover, the soldier the ideal of military heroism. The gambler stops a roll of the dice before he joins the others on a special train for people like himself, emigrants from the culture, even pilgrims.

In the second chapter of *Abwesenheit* the old man, in his slowly emerging role as Chuang-tzu's prophetic sage and teacher, offers an interesting parable to the assembled group on the "identity" of names and places. The theme of his parable relates to the unnamed destination of their unique journey. The landscape outside the train is increasingly charged with physical change and transformation – desert becoming forest, built-up cities, and abandoned roadsides. The landscape changes into cultivated land, the sea, and high mountains, all of which represent the visible world. Place names, the old man says, are only "apparently" real; they are temporary tags given by man to both real and fictional places in the present and past. The old man notes the unknown countries that must have existed, whose only reality was the name indicating their direction: north, south, east, west. Atlantis disappeared and became part of a legend. History, civilization, and cultures, the old man suggests, exist at the pleasure of the moment: "But I continue to believe that places have their own power. Those are places that are small, not large. They are unknown, abroad and at home. They have no name, distinguished only by their having nothing. Those places have power because nothing is there anymore. I believe in oases of emptiness" (*Abwesenheit*, 82).

Such an argument not only alludes to the spiritual nature of the group's train journey into "emptiness" – or the nonspecificity of destination – but suggests that an empty place portends fullness. It is enough for an adept to have simply been "there" rather than "here." The journey of the group is from "here" to "there." Names and places are temporal, and in the Eastern religious concept of the universe, nothing is static. Change "there" is an illusion, and as the old man reminds the young woman, her wish to stay somewhere forever is an impossible one, for there is no permanence in fulfillment, here or anywhere. The old man's point is, once again, that the fundamental nature of the universe is to avoid stability, that creation is renewal, a generative urge to shape and transform. The enigmatic meaning behind Handke's title *Abwesenheit* becomes clearer for the reader: in Taoism absence is a relative word, not a true opposite of fulfillment; it denotes fulfillment or a potential for fulfillment. This idea also seems to be suggested in a closing image of the second chapter – namely, the group's arrival (on foot) at a military cemetery that "magically" appears as an element of the shifting landscape. Over the grave of each soldier is a marble slab with a name and the word *present*. Here life and death are not in opposition but merely two sides of the same reality. Man is no exception to this rule of duality. Soon after this encounter, the group leaves the flat plain and

climbs to the threshold of a vast plateau, where a further stage of
their spiritual journey will continue to unfold.

This is the group's entry into a chimerical, illusory country. It
seems to be a place of prehistorical beginnings as well as a place for
the burial of cultures, an area of anticipation betraying shards of
man's past history. The area is described by the group leader as the
goal, the ultimate destination of the journey. The presence of life in
this land is nevertheless an illusion, for it is the stuff of man's dreams
and the instigator of "deceptive" images and perceptions. The old
man intimates that if the group is "new" to this place, they are not
strangers to it, since it defined them as "wanderers" in the conventional world. As "readers" they were "dreamers" and perpetual outsiders for whom this land was a goal (*Abwesenheit*, 134). Here
Handke follows the Taoist precept that books finally fail to articulate
and express the adept's (and the teacher's) felt desire for the
achievement of mystic unity. Sages, even sustaining Taoist masters,
prefer to teach through example and oral preaching. The old man
decides to hide his "accursed notebook," the arcane listing of symbols and ciphers he was compiling in the city before he undertook
this journey. He leaves the group, retreating into the desert, into
silence, the "source of images" (*Abwesenheit*, 179). Writing failed
him in his effort to apply his insights to spiritual teaching. This is a
reference to the Taoist teaching that the unity within the flow of life
is impossible to learn as public, systematized knowledge. This sentiment is noted in a key line of Handke's text, when the old man says
of himself that only in being alone did things become significant and
communicable. The old man's abandonment of the group, however,
leaves them to their own devices as they make their way back to the
European city. The soldier especially mourns the loss of a leader
who led him like a magician into a "labyrinth," the bearer of false
information (*Abwesenheit*, 217). Within the context of Eastern mysti-
cism, however, the labyrinth may be understood as a metaphor for
the soul's wandering, its longing for perfect unity.

The group's journey, though in its final stages of realization, will
last another year. Through consensus, the group will search for its
absent leader. They will find his missing notebook, whose location is
revealed to the young soldier in a dream, and they will attempt to
decipher it. In Eastern religious and spiritual fables, an adept often
begins his search for a divine teacher in a great country, enters a

barren wilderness, and moves from there into the void, where he discovers that the teacher is within his head. The missing sage of Handke's fairy tale is of that very special class. He has turned invisible owing to his perfect evolution as a great teacher, and he gives the group the unfettered gift of spiritual liberty, which is a central theme of *Abwesenheit*. They are unburdened of estrangement and alienation. An excerpt from a text by Chuang-tzu concludes Handke's book: "Man's life between heaven and earth is like a white colt dropping into a crevasse and suddenly disappearing. . . . Suppose we try to roam about in the palace of Nowhere, where all things are one" (Manheim, 119). *Abwesenheit* is an invitation to the reader to undertake such a journey under magical, fabulous auspices into a spiritual realm.

Conclusion

Peter Handke's first plays (*Sprechstücke*) were more than random examples of the literary anarchy for which he achieved notoriety at the 1966 Princeton meeting of Group 47. These plays signaled his support for theatrical experiment and Austrian postmodernist literature, which were based in Vienna and Graz and concerned with the instability of language as a valid means of communication. In Austria writers and poets trying to purge Nazi ideology from German language and literature began at point zero and stressed that there was no absolute identity between a word (the signifier) and the object to which it referred (the signified). Written in 1966-67, the *Sprechstücke* were intended to stand beyond the pale of conventional theater with its false realism and predictable structures, plots, and characterizations. These short plays also challenged Brecht's theater of alienation, which used leftist themes and audience manipulation. For young Handke, the act of writing was freely inventive, and he induced his audiences to accept theater as a form of constructed – and hence patently artificial – art. Meaning in any one of the *Sprechstücke* emerges from its visibility in ascending structures, a device through which Handke prefers to convey meaning. The *Sprechstücke* are also "language pieces" concerned with decoding the problematic character of audience-actor relations (see *Publikumsbeschimpfung*), the tautology of language (*Weissagung*), and a listing of "sins" by a narrator-speaker, who enumerates his "crimes" against the language of social conformity (*Selbstbezichtigung*).

Two longer plays that followed the *Sprechstücke*, *Kaspar* and *Der Ritt über den Bodensee*, function, as Schlueter has suggested, as dramatizations of Wittgensteinian ideas – that is, Handke's illustrations of the relationship between language and perception. *Kaspar*'s title character serves as raw material for Handke's model of language as thought control; in *Bodensee* all the characters trip and fall on the thin ice of language and rational language communication. *Das Spiel vom Fragen*, Handke's latest play, opens with a short quote from

Dante's *Vita Nuova* that underlines the writer's tone and direction in a work that is a journey of pilgrims, seven characters wandering in a land of questions, answers, and meditations. The reader and the viewer have no choice but to accept *Das Spiel vom Fragen* as a distinctly different work from its theatrical predecessors but still in line with the maturing writer's quest for artistic and philosophical self-identity. Handke refuses to assign a definite meaning to this work, which was offered at the Salzburg Festival in 1990.

The postmodernist tone of Handke's theater is matched by that of a number of prose works, novels, and short stories, which form the second major source of his artistic creativity. Handke's early prose pieces were collected in *Begrüssung des Aufsichtsrats* (1967) and *Ich bin ein Bewohner des Elfenbeinturms* (1972), the latter text a compendium of critical essays and book reviews. These prose texts, as well as his first and second novels, *Die Hornissen* and *Der Hausierer*, betray Handke's obvious borrowings from the French new novel and its declaration of independent narrative and language strategies: language devoid of description and metaphor, deconstruction of literary genres, and the parallel identity of the author as his "ideal" reader. Influences from the theoretical writings of Nathalie Sarraute and Alain Robbe-Grillet are evident at this journeyman's phase of Handke's career. In *Die Hornissen* the subject (and the narrator) is a blind man whose attempt to reconstruct his life experiences is related to a half-remembered novel that, in turn, has a blind man as its subject. In 1970 Handke was very successful with his disorienting fictional study of Joseph Bloch, a former goalkeeper turned murderer. That novel, *Die Angst des Tormanns beim Elfmeter*, is concerned with the protagonist's perception of a collapsing relationship between words and objects. *Der kurze Brief zum langen Abschied*, *Die Stunde der wahren Empfindung*, and *Die linkshändige Frau* are three subsequent examples of outsider figures devising formulas of survival within the parameters of conventional social behavior.

Wunschloses Unglück is Handke's memorial tribute to the futility of his mother's life. Her son's artistic and creative efforts fail to articulate his sorrow and grief over her death. *Langsame Heimkehr* and three related texts make up the tetralogy that was Handke's effort to shift esthetic and philosophical direction when he returned to Austria after years of self-imposed exile. *Langsame Heimkehr, Die Lehre der Sainte-Victoire*, and *Kindergeschichte*, along with the quasi-mystical prose poem *Über die Dörfer*, relate aspects of Handke's "homecoming" in poetic language and celebrate his birthplace, ethnic identity, and artistry. These texts offer their protagonists insight and guidance via the epiphanal moment, a device used, as the careful reader recalls, by writers like James Joyce and Hermann Hesse. In this sense, Handke has emerged, in language that alludes to literary models from ninteenth-century German and Austrian literature, as a curious and exceptional exponent of a latter-day romanticism. He confronts the problems of our time with "poetic" language and a call to turn inward. He is a declared admirer of Hölderlin's revival of classical art.

Handke's latest fiction, *Die Wiederholung*, *Nachmittag eines Schriftstellers*, and *Die Abwesenheit*, demonstrates both the vitality and the viability of literary genres like the bildungsroman and the fairy tale. Under the cover of the narrator's search for his missing brother in neighboring Slovenia, Handke in *Die Wiederholung* rediscovers his ethnic and artistic identity. The past illuminates the future. *Nachmittag eines Schriftstellers* is a reworking of themes clearly borrowed from F. Scott Fitgerald's short story "Afternoon of an Author." Both stories examine the writer's ability to create in a hostile society. *Die Abwesenheit*, a Taoist-inspired fairy tale, probes the meaning of a philosophical conundrum – namely, that a sense of absence denotes fulfillment. Like *Das Spiel vom Fragen*, *Die Abwesenheit* demands a spiritual awareness and an appreciation of literature as an open-ended mental construct.

In addition to drama and prose, Handke has worked in other artistic genres that reflect a broad and catholic interest: essays, journals, poetry, radio plays, and feature films. Study of all of these ancillary activities contributes to a better understanding of the writer and his creative ideas. *Versuch über die Müdigkeit* (1989; Essay about exhaustion) is an exposition on the fatigue induced by events and episodes of Handke's life. The journal *Das Gewicht der Welt* is a chronological record, set in Paris, of the author's perceptions, emotions, and consciousness; *Die Geschichte des Bleistifts* and *Phantasien der Wiederholung* (1983; Fantasies of repetition) are journals relating to the composition of the texts of the *Heimkehr* tetralogy.

Handke's most sustained effort in poetry has been the collection *Die Innenwelt der Aussenwelt der Innenwelt* (1969; The Innerworld of the outerworld of the innerworld). Poetry for Handke is an expression of the dialectic between a person's inner feelings and outward reality. The poet Handke, as critics have noted, moves the reader away from familiar ways of perceiving the inner realities of existence. This technique may involve a shift in language or the usual perspective or a change in the exterior surroundings.

Handke's radio plays were collected in a slim volume, *Wind und Meer* (1970; Wind and sea); they are actually experiments in sound and explorations of the acoustical relationships between words and sound. To date there have been no further additions to this early collection. *Die Angst des Tormanns* and *Die linkshändige Frau* have both seen the light of day as feature-length art films. The first was done under the direction of Wim Wenders, and the second was directed by Handke himself. A 1987 art-film collaboration between Handke (screenplay) and Wenders (director) was the successful *Der Himmel über Berlin*. The title, *Wings of Desire*, alludes to the imaginative setting of Berlin as a city under the protective custody of angels. Handke's 1970 television scenario, "Chronik der laufenden Ereignisse" (Chronicle of current events), is a semifictional reconstruction of television news and events; it remains an interesting but unique instance of Handke's involvement with television art.

As Klinkowitz and Knowlton have noted, Handke's position in the European and Austrian constellation of postmodernist writing is as secure as ever (128), owing to his demonstrated evolution and development without the sterility and rejection that postmodernist esthetics often inspires in the reading public. Handke redirected himself (and the reader) toward "a new phenomenology of the 'I' as a perceiving and knowing subject immersed in a threatening world" (Klinkowitz and Knowlton, 13). This positive process began with the *Heimkehr* tetralogy, in which the author offers the reader a way out of the dead end of linguistic and esthetic nihilism. Social intercourse and language once more made a subjective and luminous contact with the outer world. Handke demonstrated the way to a new beginning, to achieving a highly stylized harmony within contemporary fragmented experience, which has been the burden and the gift of the postmodernist temper. Each of Handke's subsequent texts affirms that condition yet renders it provisional as the writer's art manages to rebuild reality once again.

Notes and References

Preface

1. Jerome Klinkowitz and James Knowlton, *Peter Handke and the Postmodern Transformation* (Columbia: University of Missouri Press, 1983), vi; hereafter cited in text.

Chapter One

1. Franz Hohler, "Fragen an Peter Handke," in *Fragen an andere: Interviews mit Wolf Biermann, Peter Handke, Ernst Jandl, Mane Matte, Hannes Wader* (Bern: Zytlogge, 1973), 20; hereafter cited in text.

2. Peter Demetz, *After the Fires: Recent Writing in the Germanies, Austria, and Switzerland* (New York: Harcourt Brace Jovanovich, 1986), 214; hereafter cited in text.

3. "Ein autobiographischer Essay, 1957," in *Ich bin ein Bewohner des Elfenbeinturms* (Frankfurt: Suhrkamp, 1972), 11-16; hereafter cited in text as "Essay."

4. Heinz Ludwig Arnold, "Gespräch mit Peter Handke," *Text und Kritik* 24/24a (September 1976): 15-37; hereafter cited in text.

5. Michael Springer, "Im Internat," in *Über Peter Handke*, ed. Michael Scharang (Frankfurt: Suhrkamp, 1972), 185; hereafter cited in text.

6. Alfred Holzinger, "Peter Handkes literarische Anfänge in Graz," in *Wie die Grazer auszogen, die Literatur zu erobern*, ed. Peter Laemmle and Jörg Drews (Munich: Lipp, 1975), 183; hereafter cited in text.

7. Manfred Mixner, "Ausbruch aus der Provinz," in Laemmle and Drews, *Wie die Grazer auszogen*, 13.

8. Horst-Dieter Ebert, "Unerschrocken naiv," *Der Spiegel*, 25 May 1970, 174-90.

9. Charles Linder, "Die Ausbeutung des Bewusstseins," in *Schreiben und Leben: Gespraäche mit Jürgen Becker, Peter Handke, Walter Kempowski, Wolfgang Koeppen, Günter Wolloff, Dieter Wellershoff* (Cologne: Kiepenheuer and Witsch, 1974), 33.

10. Karin Kathrein, "Schreiben bannte die Angst," *Die Presse*, 18-19 October 1972, 7.

11. Hans Haider, "Vision von Österreich," *Die Presse*, 18 July 1978, n.p.

12. Haider, "Vision von Österreich."

13. Norbert Gabriel, *Peter Handke und Österreich* (Bonn: Bouvier, 1983); hereafter cited in text. Gabriel discusses Handke's conscious, intentional identification with Austrian history and culture.

14. June Schlueter, *The Plays and Novels of Peter Handke* (Pittsburgh: University of Pittsburgh Press, 1981), 174; hereafter cited in text.

Chapter Two

1. *Publikumsbeschimpfung*, in *Stücke I* (Frankfurt: Suhrkamp, 1972), 9-47; hereafter cited in text as *Publikumsbeschimpfung*.

2. My discussion of Handke's *Sprechstücke* is based on the following standard critical presentations: Klinkowitz and Knowlton, 104-12; Schlueter 1981, 17-40; Nicholas Hern, *Peter Handke* (New York: Ungar, 1972), 21-51, hereafter cited in text; Ronald Hayman, *Theater and Anti-theater* (New York: Oxford University Press, 1979), 95-104, hereafter cited in text; Michael Hays, "Peter Handke and the End of the 'Modern,'" *Modern Drama* 23, no. 4 (January 1981): 346-66, hereafter cited in text; Rainer Nägele, "Peter Handke: The Staging of Language," *Modern Drama* 23, no. 4 (January 1981): 327-38, hereafter cited in text; Uwe Schultz, *Peter Handke* (Velber bei Hannover: Friedrich, 1973), 25-42, hereafter cited in text.

3. *Die Weissagung*, in *Stücke I*, 49-63; hereafter cited in text as *Weissagung*. *Selbstbezichtigung*, in *Stücke I*, 65-88; hereafter cited in text as *Selbstbezichtigung*. *Hilferufe*, in *Stücke I*, 89-97; hereafter cited in text as *Hilferufe*.

4. This can be found in Handke's note to *Offending the Audience* and *Self-Accusation*, in *Kaspar and Other Plays*, trans. Michael Roloff (New York: Farrar, Straus & Giroux, 1969), v. Handke's criticism that Brecht worked within a false theatrical framework is found in Nicholas Hern's translation of Handke's essay, "Brecht, Play, Theatre, Agitation," *Theatre Quarterly* 1 (October-December 1971): 89-90. See also Hayes, 350.

5. On the Vienna Group, see Michael Butler, "From the 'Wiener Gruppe' to Ernst Jandl," in *Modern Austrian Writing*, ed. Alan Best and Hans Wolfschütz (London: Wolff, 1980), 236-51. On the Graz Group (the literary-artistic successor to the Vienna Group), see Hugh Rorrison, "The 'Grazer Gruppe,'" in Best and Wolfschütz, *Modern Austrian Writing*, 252-65; hereafter cited in text.

6. Claus Peymann, "Directing Handke," *Drama Review* 16 (June 1972): 48-49; hereafter cited in text.

7. Arthur Joseph, "Nauseated by Language," *Drama Review* 15, no 1 (Fall 1970): 59; hereafter cited in text.

8. There are outstanding discussions of *Weissagung* in Nägele, 329-31, and Schlueter 1981, 24-30.

9. "Theater and Film: The Misery of Comparison," trans. Donald Vordberg, in *Focus on Film and Theatre*, ed. James Hurt (Englewood Cliffs, N.J.: Prentice-Hall, 1974), 165; originally published in German as "Theater und Film: Das Elend der Vergleiches," in *Prosa Gedichte Theaterstücke Horspiel Aufsätze* (Frankfurt: Suhrkamp, 1969), 314-26.

10. "The play may be a demonstration of the spatial and verbal distance between the speakers on stage and the audience – a signal of the need to establish a community of support" (Hays, 356). See also Hern, 52.

11. *Kaspar*, in *Stücke I*; hereafter cited in text as *Kaspar*.

12. I have relied on the following substantial discussions of *Kaspar* in English: Denis Calandra, *New German Dramatists* (London: Macmillan, 1983), 63-74, hereafter cited in text: Hays, 356-58; Hern, 58-72; Hayman, 104-07; Linda Hill, "Obscurantism and Verbal Resistance in Handke's *Kaspar*," *Germanic Review* 53, no. 4 (1977): 304-15, hereafter cited in text; June Schlueter, " 'Goats and Monkeys' and 'Idiocy of Language': Handke's *Kaspar* and Shakespeare's *Othello*," *Modern Drama* 23, no. 1 (March 1980): 25-31. In German: Christa K. Dixon, "Peter Handkes *Kaspar*: Ein Modellfall," *German Quarterly* 46, no. 1 (January 1973): 31-46; Schultz, 43-59.

13. "Der Jasager und die Einsager," in Scharang, 132.

14. See R. D. Theisz, "Kaspar Hauser im zwanzigsten Jahrhundert," *German Quarterly* 49, no. 2 (March 1976): 168-79.

15. "The play provides no specific answer to the problem of linguistic oppression" (Hays, 357).

16. *Das Mündel will Vormund sein*, in *Stücke II* (Frankfurt: Suhrkamp, 1973), 7-38; hereafter cited in text as *Mündel*. *Quodlibet*, in *Stücke II*, 39-54; hereafter cited in text as *Quodlibet*.

17. "*My Foot My Tutor* . . . is a play of form, not meaning" (Hays, 358). Other discussions of *Mündel* that I have found helpful are Nägele, 334-35; Calandra, 31-43; Haymann, 110-13; Peymann, 52-53; Bonnie Marranca, "Peter Handke's *My Foot My Tutor*: Aspects of Modernism," *Michigan Quarterly Review* 16 (1977): 272-79, hereafter cited in text; Schultz, 60-72.

18. Hern (84) and Marranca (274) both cite the influence on *Mündel* of Beckett's *Act without Words* (1957).

19. Carl Weber, "Handke's Stage Is a Laboratory," *Drama Review* 162 (June 1972): 56; hereafter cited in text.

20. Helpful to an understanding of *Quodlibet* are Calandra, 56-60; Handke, "Zur Aufführung von *Quodlibet*," in *Stücke II*, 157-59; Peter Hamm, "Handke entdeckt sich selbst," in Scharang, 157-62; Rainer Litten, "Theater der Verstörung: Ein Gespräch mit Peter Handke," in Scharang, 157-58.

21. Translator's note to *Quodlibet*, in *The Ride across Lake Constance and Other Plays*, trans. Michael Roloff (New York: Farrar, Strauss & Giroux, 1976), 55.

22. "The success of the play depends on the audience's predictable association and responses" (Schlueter 1981, 61).

23. *Der Ritt über den Bodensee*, in *Stücke II*, 55-154; hereafter cited in text as *Bodensee*.

24. See Handke's introduction to *Stücke II*, 57-59, and "Aus den Notizen zu *Der Ritt über den Bodensee*," his outline listing of notes to the writing of the play. These notes are in fact a scenario of actors' movements and gestures; movements are also interpreted (*Stücke II*, 161-77).

25. The title of the play comes from an 1828 German Swabian romantic ballad, "Der Reiter und der Bodensee" (The Rider and Lake Constance), by Gustav Schwab (1792-1850), in which a horseman dies when he hears that his perilous ride across the thin ice of Lake Constance was in fact a chance event of nature. For Handke, this is also an encounter with the "thin ice" of rationality. Recommended discussion of *Bodensee* are June Schlueter, "Handke's *The Ride across Lake Constance*," in *Metafictional Characters in Modern Drama* (New York: Columbia University Press, 1979), 105-19; Michael Linstead, *Outer World and Inner World: Socialization and Emancipation in the Works of Peter Handke, 1964-1981*, European Literary Studies, German Languages and Literature Series, vol. 1024 (Frankfurt: Lang, 1988), 71-81, hereafter cited in text; Schultz, 77-86.

26. Carl Weber directed the American premiere of *Bodensee* on 13 January 1972 at the Forum Theater at Lincoln Center in New York. His article "Handke's Stage Is a Laboratory" contains his notes relating to that production, which had a bad house. See, however, another analysis of the American premiere in Ira Hauptmann, "Aspects of Handke: A Play," *Partisan Review* 45, no. 3 (1978): 425-30.

27. For example, the characters Jannings and George "act out" the features of a prototypical master-servant relationship. Bergner, Stroheim, and Porten symbolize a destabilized lovers' triangle.

28. *Die Unvernünftigen sterben aus* (Frankfurt: Suhrkamp, 1973); hereafter cited in text as *Unvernünftigen*. The English title of the play omits the German word *Unvernünftigen* ("irrational ones").

29. The Yale production is discussed in Mark Bly, "Theater in New Haven: Weber on Handke," *Theater* 11, no. 2 (Spring 1980): 83-87; hereafter cited in text. Other productions are discussed in Calandra, 83-90; June Schlueter, "Politics and Poetry: Peter Handke's *They Are Dying Out*," *Modern Drama* 23, no. 4 (January 1981): 339-45; Linstead 1988, 136-48; Schultz, 86-103. Hellmuth Karasek, reviewing the Zürich production in *Der Spiegel* (22 April 1974), said it was ironic that Handke's protagonist, Quitt, should have a precedent in Brecht's drama since Handke professed to despise Brecht's theater.

30. Christian Schulz-Gerstein, "Das Leiden als Geschäfts-Trick: Gespräch mit Peter Handke über sein Stück," *Die Zeit*, 26 April 1974.

31. "As opposed to political engagement, Handke opposes a poetic utopia, in which he sees the possibility of becoming a poetic, i.e., an unnatural man" (Arnold Blumer, "Peter Handkes Romantische Unvernunft," *Acta Germanica* 8 [1973]: 126; hereafter cited in text). A similar discussion is found in Arnold, 29-31.

32. Joseph A. Federico, "The Hero as Playwright in Dramas by Frisch, Dürrenmatt, and Handke," *German Life and Letters*, n.s. 32 (January 1979): 166; hereafter cited in text.

33. The German text of the speech, entitled "Die Geborgenheit unter der Schädeldecke," is found in *Als das Wünschen noch geholfen hat* (Frankfurt: Suhrkamp, 1974), 71.

34. Schlueter, "Politics," 343.

Chapter Three

1. *Begrübung des Aufsichfsrats: Prosatexte* (Salzburg: Residenz, 1967), 5.

2. "Ich bin ein Bewohner des Elfenbeinturms," in *Ich bin ein Bewohner des Elfenbeinturms* (Frankfurt: Suhrkamp, 1972), 22; hereafter cited in text as *Bewohner*.

3. Manfred Mixner, *Peter Handke* (Kronberg: Athenäum, 1977), 51; hereafter cited in text.

4. Dieter Zimmer, cited in *Gruppe 47: Bericht, Kritik, Polemik: Ein Handbuch*, ed. Reinard Lettau (Neuwied and Berlin: Luchterhand, 1967), 233. The date of Zimmer's article is 6 May 1966.

5. "Zur Tagung der Gruppe 47," in *Bewohner*, 29-34; hereafter cited in text as "Tagung."

6. "Die Literatur ist romantisch," in *Bewohner*, 35-50; hereafter cited in text as "Literatur."

7. Michael Linstead, "Peter Handke," in *The Modern German Novel*, ed. Keith Bullivant (Leamington Spa: Berg Publishers, 1987), 156; hereafter cited in text.

8. Besides living extensively in Paris, Handke has translated the French writers Emmanuel Bove, René Char, and Marguerite Duras into German.

9. Alain Robbe-Grillet, *For a New Novel: Essays on Fiction* (1962), trans. Richard Howard (New York: Grove Press, 1965); hereafter cited in text. Nathalie Sarraute, *The Age of Suspicion: Essays on the Novel* (1956), trans. Maria Jolas (New York: George Braziller, 1963); hereafter cited in text. Further discussion of the Handke – Robbe-Grillet relationship is found in Linstead 1988, 31-35: "The most striking forerunner of Handke comes from France in the shape of the *nouveau roman* and its fervent practitioner and theorist Alain Robbe-Grillet" (31).

10. *Die Hornissen* (Frankfurt: Suhrkamp, 1966); hereafter cited in text as *Hornissen*. The 1978 Suhrkamp edition was shortened by the author.

11. Recommended discussions in English: Thomas F. Barry, "In Search of Lost Texts: Memory and the Existential Quest in Peter Handke's *Die Hornissen*," *Seminar* 19, no. 3 (September 1983): 194-214, hereafter cited in text; David Darby, "The Narrative Text as Palimpsest: Levels of Discourse in Peter Handke's *Die Hornissen*," *Seminar* 23, no. 3 (September 1987): 251-64, hereafter cited in text. Recommended discussions in German: Mixner 1977, 1-26; Gabriel, 49-53.

12. Hans Widrich, "*Die Hornissen* – auch ein Mosaik aus Unterkärnten," in *Peter Handke*, ed. Raimund Fellinger (Frankfurt: Suhrkamp, 1985), 25-35; hereafter cited in text.

13. Especially helpful to me here are ideas garnered from a reading of Roland Barthes, "The Structuralist Activity," in *Critical Essays*, trans. Richard Howard (Evanston, Ill.: Northwestern University Press, 1972), 213-20; hereafter cited in text.

14. *Der Hausierer* (Frankfurt: Suhrkamp, 1967); hereafter cited in text as *Hausierer*.

15. "Über meinen neuen Roman *Der Hausierer*," in Fellinger, 37. In this two-page statement on the structure and theory behind the novel, Handke instructs the reader to "find his *own* story" within reflective sentences.

16. *Die Angst des Tormanns beim Elfmeter* (Frankfurt: Suhrkamp, 1970); hereafter cited in text as *Angst*. German-language reviews can be found in Fellinger, 406-10. For English-language reviews, see, among others, Stanley Kauffmann, "Inside Out," *World*, 18 July 1972, 62-65, hereafter cited in text; and A. Leslie Wilson in *Books Abroad* (Winter 1972): 107.

17. Full details and discussions of Wenders's adaptation can be found in Peter Brunette, "Filming Words: Wenders's *The Goalie's Anxiety at the Penalty Kick* (1971)," in *Modern European Filmmakers and the Art of Adaptation*, ed. Andrew Horton and Joan Magretta (New York: Ungar, 1981), 188-202; and Kathe Geist, *The Cinema of Wim Wenders: From Paris, France, to Paris, Texas* (Ann Arbor: UMI Research Press, 1988), 20.

18. Jerome Klinkowitz, "Aspekte der Prosa Peter Handkes," in Fellinger, 38.

19. Recommended critical studies that form the background of my discussion are Linda C. DeMeritt, *New Subjectivity and Prose: Peter Handke and Botho Strauss* (New York: Lang, 1987), 152: Linstead 1988, 88; J. J. White, "Signs of Disturbance: The Semiological Import of Some Recent Fiction by Michel Tournier and Peter Handke," *Journal of European Studies* 4 (1974): 233-54; hereafter cited in text.

20. Schlueter (1988, 85) discusses the novel's kinship to Kafka, who, like Handke, may be more concerned with meaning per se than with the nature of the world.

21. *Der kurze Brief zum langen Abschied* (Frankfurt: Suhrkamp, 1972); hereafter cited in text as *Brief.*

22. Helmuth Karasek, "Ohne zu verallgemeinern: Ein Gespräch mit Peter Handke," in Scharang, 85.

23. Bruno Hillebrand, "Auf der Suche nach der verlorenen Identität: Peter Handkes *Der kurze Brief zum langen Abschied,*" in *Der deutsche Roman im 20: Jahrhundert,* vol. 2, ed. Manfred Brauneck (Bamberg: Buchners, 1976), 101.

24. Schlueter 1981, 95, 102; see especially Christine Kraus, "Literarische Vorbilder in Peter Handkes Roman *Der kurze Brief zum langen Abschied,*" *Österreich in Geschichte und Literatur* 24 (May-June 1978): 174-80. The American reception of Peter Handke's work in general is discussed by Thomas F. Barry, "America Reflected: On the American Reception of Peter Handke's Writings/Handke's Reception of America in His Writings," *Modern Austrian Literature* 20, no. 314 (1987): 107-15; hereafter cited in text.

25. A slightly different interpretation of Handke's "another time" is offered by Jürgen Kleist, "Die Akzeptanz des Gegebenen: Zur Problematik des Künstlers in Peter Handkes *Der kurze Brief zum langen Abschied,*" *Modern Austrian Literature* 21, no. 2 (1988): 95-103. Kleist argues that the "artist" (the narrator in *Brief*) settles for the "given" rather than the "utopian" vision of life as a way out of his existentialist dilemma (100).

26. "The book's dual process of reality and 'John Ford' parareality, its duality of European and American cultures are structurally aligned to the dual theme at the center: fear – of existence itself – that the narrator brings from Europe, along with a perspective on that fear that he gains in America" (Stanley Kauffmann, review of *Der kurze Brief zum langen Abschied, New Republic,* 28 September 1974, 30).

Chapter Four

1. *Wunschloses Unglück* (Salzburg: Residenz, 1972); hereafter cited in text as *Unglück.*

2. Ralph Manheim translates Handke's German subtitle *Erzählung* – which literally denotes a "telling," mostly within a fictional context – as "A Life Story." I prefer to think of *Unglück* as a special instance of biography.

3. These segments suggested in William H. Rey, "Provokation durch den Tod, Peter Handkes Erzählung *Wunschloses Unglück* als Modell stilistischer Integration," *German Studies Review* 1 (October 1978): 286-87.

4. Helmut Scheffel, review of *Wunschloses Unglück*, in *Frankfurter Allgemeine Zeitung*, 4 November 1972. See also Frank Kermode's review of *Unglück*, "The Model of the Modern Modernist," *New York Review of Books*, 1 May 1975, 20-23; hereafter cited in text.

5. David H. Miles calls this recurrent stylistic device an example of Handke's progressive ("changing") realism, a realism of linguistic defamiliarization ("Reality and the Two Realisms: Mimesis in Auerbach, Lukács and Handke" *Monatshefte* 71, 4 [1979]: 377; hereafter cited in text).

6. *Die Stunde der wahren Empfindung* (Frankfurt: Suhrkamp, 1975); hereafter cited in text as *Stunde*.

7. "There is *no* reason why Handke chose these particular objects, because their existence as particular objects is not important" (Linstead 1988, 16). Chance governs the appearance of the "moment."

8. *Die linkshändige Frau* (Frankfurt: Suhrkamp Verlag, 1976); hereafter cited in the text as *Frau*.

9. J. Hobermann, review of *Frau*, *Village Voice*, 7 April 1980; Roger Angell, review of *Frau*, *New Yorker*, 28 April 1980.

10. *Falsche Bewegung* (screenplay) (Frankfurt: Suhrkamp, 1975). For an English discussion of this film, see Peter Harcourt, " 'Adaptation through Inversion': Wenders's *Wrong Moment* (1974)," in Horton and Magretta, *Modern European Filmmakers*, 263-77.

11. Stanley Kauffmann, review of *The Left-Handed Woman*, *Nation*, 8 March 1980.

12. "Durch eine Mythische Tür eintreten," reprinted in Fellinger, 234-41; hereafter cited in text. To my knowledge, the essay has not been published in English.

13. Eberhard Frey, *World Literature Today* 51 (Autumn 1977): 608, hereafter cited in text; Mixner, 231.

14. Siegfried Schober, " 'Es soll mythisch sein, mythisch!' " *Der Spiegel*, 2 May 1977, 177-80 (quoted in Mixner, 231).

Chapter Five

1. *Slow Homecoming*, including *The Long Way Around*, *The Lesson of Mont Saint-Victoire*, and *Child Story*, trans. Ralph Manheim (New York: Farrar, Straus & Giroux, 1985).

2. *Langsame Heimkehr* (Frankfurt: Suhrkamp, 1979); hereafter cited in text as *Heimkehr*.

3. *Die Lehre der Sainte-Victoire* (Frankfurt: Suhrkamp, 1980); hereafter cited in text as *Saint-Victoire*.

4. *Kindergeschichte* (Frankfurt: Suhrkamp, 1981); hereafter cited in text as *Kindergeschichte*. *Über die Dörfer: Dramatisches Gedicht* (Frankfurt: Suhrkamp, 1981); hereafter cited in text as *Dörfer*.

5. Especially Linda C. DeMeritt, "Peter Handke: From Alienation to Orientation," *Modern Austrian Literature* 20, no. 1 (1987): 61, hereafter cited in text; and Francis M. Sharp, "Peter Handke," in *Major Figures of Contemporary Austrian Literature*, ed. Donald G. Daviau (New York: Lang, 1987), 224, hereafter cited in text.

6. Blumer's "Peter Handkes romantische Unvernunft" is an extended, substantial discussion.

7. Frank Elgar, *Cézanne* (New York: Abrams, 1975), 141-42.

8. Amina appears as "A" in Handke's first journal, *Das Gewicht der Welt*, which is based on his life in Paris.

9. Peter Pütz, *Peter Handke* (Frankfurt: Suhrkamp, 1982), 116.

10. Rolf Günter Renner, *Peter Handke* (Stuttgart: Metzler, 1985), 139; hereafter cited in text.

11. Rolf Michaelis, "Himmelwärts," *Die Zeit*, 13 August 1982; Hilde Spiel, "Handkes festliche Heilsbotschaft," *Frankfurter Allgemeine Zeitung*, 10 August 1982.

12. Krista Fleischmann, "Ein Gespräch über das Schreiben und die *Kindergeschichte*," *Die Rampe* 2 (1981): 7-15; hereafter cited in text. *Die Geschichte des Bleistifts* (Salzburg: Residenz, 1982); hereafter cited in text as *Geschichte*. This journal of Handke's is a good source for discussion of the tetralogy's composition.

13. Doris Runzheimer, *Peter Handkes Wendung zur Geschichte* (Frankfurt: Lang, 1987), 282-83.

14. Herbert Gamper, *Peter Handke: Aber ich lebe nur von den Zwischenräumen* (Zürich: Amman, 1987), 99; hereafter cited in text.

Chapter Six

1. *Der Chinese des Schmerzes* (Frankfurt: Suhrkamp, 1983); hereafter cited in text as *Chinese*.

2. Renner's chapter on *Chinese* is basic to my reading of Handke's novel.

3. *Die Wiederholung* (Frankfurt: Suhrkamp, 1986); hereafter cited in text as *Wiederholung*.

4. David Pryce-Jones, review of *Die Wiederholung*, *New York Times Book Review*, 7 August 1988. The word *bildungsroman* is used by Filip in *Wiederholung*.

5. Ralph Sassone ("Brotherland," *Village Voice*, 14 June 1988) suggests that *Wiederholung* is ultimately as much Gregor's story as it is his brother's.

6. *Nachmittag eines Schriftstellers* (Salzburg: Residenz, 1987); hereafter cited in text as *Nachmittag*. F. Scott Fitzgerald, "Afternoon of an Author," in *Afternoon of an Author: A Selection of Unpublished Stories and*

Essays, ed. Arthur Mizener (New York: Charles Scribner's Sons, 1957), 177-82; hereafter cited in text as Mizener.

7. John Updike, review of *Nachmittag eines Schriftstellers*, *New Yorker*, 25 December 1989, 108.

8. *Die Abwesenheit: Ein Märchen* (Frankfurt: Suhrkamp, 1987); hereafter cited in text as *Abwesenheit*. *Märchen* translates as "fairy tale."

9. *Absence*, trans. Ralph Manheim (New York: Farrar, Straus & Giroux, 1990), v; hereafter cited in text as Manheim.

Selected Bibliography

PRIMARY WORKS

German Editions

Novels

Die Abwesenheit: Ein Märchen. Frankfurt: Suhrkamp, 1987.
Die Angst des Tormanns beim Elfmeter. Frankfurt: Suhrkamp, 1970.
Der Chinese des Schmerzes. Frankfurt: Suhrkamp, 1983.
Der Hausierer. Frankfurt: Suhrkamp, 1967.
Die Hornissen. Frankfurt: Suhrkamp, 1966.
Kindergeschichte. Frankfurt: Suhrkamp, 1981.
Der kurze Brief zum langen Abschied. Frankfurt: Suhrkamp, 1972.
Langsame Heimkehr. Frankfurt: Suhrkamp, 1979.
Die Lehre der Sainte-Victoire. Frankfurt: Suhrkamp, 1980.
Die linkshändige Frau. Frankfurt: Suhrkamp, 1976.
Nachmittag eines Schriftstellers. Salzburg: Residenz, 1987.
Die Stunde der wahren Empfindung. Frankfurt: Suhrkamp, 1975.
Die Wiederholung. Frankfurt: Suhrkamp, 1986.

Poetry

Das Ende des Flanierens. Wien: David Messe/Hermann Gail, 1977.
Deutsche Gedichte. Frankfurt: Euphorion, 1969.
Gedichte. Frankfurt: Suhrkamp, 1987.
Gedicht an die Dauer. Frankfurt: Suhrkamp, 1986.
Die Innenwelt der Aussenwelt der Innenwelt. Frankfurt: Suhrkamp, 1969.

Plays

Hilferufe. In *Stücke I*. Frankfurt: Suhrkamp, 1972.
Kaspar. In *Stücke I*. Frankfurt: Suhrkamp, 1972.
Das Mündel will Vormund sein. In *Stücke II*. Frankfurt: Suhrkamp, 1973.
Publikumsbeschimpfung. In *Stücke I*. Frankfurt: Suhrkamp, 1972.
Quodlibet. In *Stücke II*. Frankfurt: Suhrkamp, 1973.
Der Ritt über den Bodensee. In *Stücke II*. Frankfurt: Suhrkamp, 1973.

Selbstbezichtigung. In *Stücke I*. Frankfurt: Suhrkamp, 1972.

Das Spiel vom Fragen. Frankfurt: Suhrkamp, 1989.

Über die Dörfer: Dramatisches Gedicht. Frankfurt: Suhrkamp, 1981.

Die Unvernünftigen sterben aus. Frankfurt: Suhrkamp, 1973.

Die Weissagung. In *Stücke I*. Frankfurt: Suhrkamp, 1972.

Radio Plays

Hörspiel. In *wdr-Hörspielbuch 1968*. Cologne: Kiepenheuer and Witsch, 1968.

Hörspiel 2. In *wdr-Hörspielbuch 1969*. Cologne: Kiepenheuer and Witsch, 1968.

Hörspiel 2, 3, und 4. Frankfurt: Verlag der Autoren, 1970.

Wind und Meer: Vier Hörspiele. Frankfurt: Suhrkamp, 1970. Includes *Geräusch eines Geräusches* and *Wind und Meer*.

Film and Television Scripts

Die Angst des Tormanns beim Elfmeter (with Wim Wenders). 1972. Directed by Wim Wenders. Feature film.

"Chronik der laufenden Ereignisse." 1971. Directed by Peter Handke. Television film.

3 amerikanische LP's. 1969. Directed by Wim Wenders. Short film.

Falsche Bewegung. 1975. Based on Goethe's novel *Wilhelm Meisters Lehrjahre*. Directed by Wim Wenders. Feature film.

Der Himmel über Berlin (with Wim Wenders). 1987. Directed by Wim Wenders. Feature film.

Die linkshändige Frau. 1977. Directed by Peter Handke. Feature film.

Translations

Aeschylus. *Prometheus Bound*. Frankfurt: Suhrkamp, 1986.

Char, René. *Le Nu perdu*. München: Carl Hanser, 1984.

Lipus, Florjan. *Der Zögling Tjaz*. With Helga Mracnikar. Salzburg: Residenz, 1981.

Percy, Walker. *The Moviegoer*. Frankfurt: Suhrkamp, 1980.

Collections

Als das Wünschen noch geholfen hat. Frankfurt: Suhrkamp, 1974. Poems, essays, photographs.

Begrüssung des Aufsichsrats: Prosatexte. Salzburg: Residenz, 1967. Short stories.

Das Ende des Flanierens: Gedichte, Aufsätze, Reden Rezensionern. Frankfurt: Suhrkamp, 1984. Essays, poems, speeches.

Prosa Gedichte Theaterstücke Hörspiel Aufsätze. Frankfurt: Suhrkamp, 1969. Short stories, poems, the plays *Publikumsbeschimfung* and *Das Mündel will Vormund sein,* a radio play, and several essays.

Publikumsbeschimpfung und andere Sprechstücke. Frankfurt: Suhrkamp, 1966. Contains the plays *Publikumsbeschimpfung, Die Weissagung,* and *Selbstbezichtigung.*

Der Rand der Wörter: Erzählungen Gedichte Stücke. Edited by Heinz F. Schafroth. Stuttgart: Reclam, 1975. Short stories, poems, and the plays *Die Weissagung, Hilferufe,* and *Quodlibet.*

Stücke I. Frankfurt: Suhrkamp, 1972. Contains the plays *Publikums-beschimpfung, Die Weissagung, Selbstbezichtigung, Hilferufe,* and *Kaspar.*

Stücke II. Frankfurt: Suhrkamp, 1973. Contains the plays *Das Mündel will Vormund sein, Quodlibet,* and *Der Ritt über den Bodensee.*

Nonfiction

Die Geschichte des Bleistifts. Salzburg: Residenz, 1982. Journals.

Das Gewicht der Welt: Ein Journal. Salzburg: Residenz, 1977. Journals.

Ich bin ein Bewohner des Elfenbeinturms. Frankfurt: Suhrkamp, 1972. Essays.

Die Literatur ist romantisch. Berlin: Oberbammpresse, 1967. Essays.

Phantasien der Wiederholung. Frankfurt: Suhrkamp, 1983. Journals.

Versuch über die Jukebox. Frankfurt: Suhrkamp, 1990. Essays.

Versuch über die Müdigkeit. Frankfurt: Suhrkamp, 1989. Essays.

Wunschloses Unglück. Salzburg: Residenz, 1972. Memoir.

Other

Der gewöhnliche Schrecken: Horrorgeschichten. Salzburg: Residenz, 1969. Short-story collection edited by Handke.

Walter Pichler: Skulpturen, Zeichnungen, Modelle. Frankfurt: Die Gallerie, 1987. Text by Handke to a catalog of an exhibition of the artist's work.

Wiener Läden, mit Sätzen von Peter Handke. Munich: Hauser, 1974. Prose accompanying the art of Didi Petrikat.

English Translations

Novels

Absence. Translated by Ralph Manheim. New York: Farrar, Straus & Giroux, 1990.

Across. Translated by Ralph Manheim. New York: Farrar, Straus & Giroux, 1986.

The Afternoon of a Writer. Translated by Ralph Manheim. New York: Farrar, Straus & Giroux, 1989.

The Goalie's Anxiety at the Penalty Kick. Translated by Michael Roloff. New York: Farrar, Straus & Giroux, 1972.

The Left-Handed Woman. Translated by Ralph Manheim. New York: Farrar, Straus & Giroux, 1978.

A Moment of True Feeling. Translated by Ralph Manheim. New York: Farrar, Straus & Giroux, 1977.

Repetition. Translated by Ralph Manheim. New York: Farrar, Straus & Giroux, 1988.

Short Letter, Long Farewell. Translated by Ralph Manheim. New York: Farrar, Straus & Giroux, 1974.

Poetry

The Innerworld of the Outerworld of the Innerworld. Translated by Michael Roloff. New York: Seabury Press, 1974.

Nonsense and Happiness. Translated by Michael Roloff. New York: Urizen Books, 1976.

Plays

Kaspar and Other Plays. Translated by Michael Roloff. New York: Farrar, Straus & Giroux, 1969. Contains *Offending the Audience*, *Self-Accusation*, and *Kaspar*.

The Ride across Lake Constance and Other Plays. Translated by Michael Roloff. New York: Farrar, Straus & Giroux, 1976. Contains *Prophecy*, *Calling for Help*, *My Foot My Tutor*, *Quodlibet*, *The Ride across Lake Constance*, and *They Are Dying Out*.

Nonfiction

A Sorrow beyond Dreams. Translated by Ralph Manheim. New York: Farrar, Straus & Giroux, 1974. Memoir.

The Weight of the World. Translated by Ralph Manheim. New York: Farrar, Straus & Giroux, 1984. Journal.

Collections

Slow Homecoming. Translated by Ralph Manheim. New York: Farrar, Straus & Giroux, 1985. Contains *The Long Way Around*, *The Lesson of Mont Sainte-Victoire*, and *Child Story*.

Three by Peter Handke. Translated by Michael Roloff and Ralph Manheim. New York: Farrar, Straus & Giroux, 1977. Contains *The Goalie's Anxiety at the Penalty Kick*, *Short Letter, Long Farewell*, and *A Sorrow beyond Dreams*.

Two Novels by Peter Handke. Translated by Ralph Manheim. New York: Farrar, Straus & Giroux, 1979. Contains *A Moment of True Feeling* and *The Left-handed Woman*.

SECONDARY WORKS

Interviews

" 'Der Alltag ist schändlich leblos.' Interview with Hellmuth Karasek and Willi Winkler." *Der Spiegel*, 16 April 1990, 220-34. Recent interview with Handke.

Arnold, Heinz Ludwig, "Gespräch mit Peter Handke." *Text und Kritik* 24/24a (September 1976): 15-37. Interview with Handke conducted in Paris on 29 September 1975.

Gamper, Herbert. *Peter Handke: Aber ich lebe nur von den Zwischenräumen: Ein Gespräch*. Zürich: Amman, 1978. Extensive, little-known 1986 interview with Handke in Salzburg, his home territory, along with discussions of his recent novels.

Hohler, Franz, ed. "Fragen an Peter Handke." In *Fragen an andere: Interviews mit Wolf Biermann, Peter Handke, Ernst Jandl, Mani Matte, Hannes Wader*, 19-39. Bern: Zytglogge, 1973. An early (1972) interview with Handke in Kronberg.

Schlueter, June, ed. *The Plays and Novels of Peter Handke*. Pittsburgh: University of Pittsburgh Press, 1981. Contains her interview with Handke.

Books

Calandra, Denis. *New German Dramatists*. London: Macmillan, 1983. Three chapters on Handke's plays discuss the works alone and in context with his German-language contemporaries.

Fellinger, Raimund, ed. *Peter Handke*. Frankfurt: Suhrkamp, 1985. Standard general collection of interpretative essays in German by many critics of Handke's writings through the *Heimkehr* tetralogy.

Gabriel, Norbert. *Peter Handke und Österreich*. Bonn: Bouvier, 1983. Looks at Austria as the setting in Handke's work.

Geist, Kathe. *The Cinema of Wim Wenders*. Studies in Cinema, no. 41. Ann Arbor: UMI Research Press, 1988. Very helpful on both Wenders and Handke as filmmakers.

Hern, Nicholas. *Peter Handke*. New York: Ungar, 1972. Intended as a brief survey of Handke the playwright, the book highlights central interpretative issues. One of the few Handke monographs available in English.

Klinkowitz, Jerome, and James Knowlton. *Peter Handke and the Postmodern Transformation*. Columbia: University of Missouri Press, 1983.

Handke's work discussed through 1981 within the wider context of postmodernist esthetics. Guidebook format.

Linstead, Michael. *Outer World and Inner World: Socialization and Emancipation in the Works of Peter Handke, 1964-1981*. European Literary Studies, German Languages and Literature Series, vol. 1024. Frankfurt: Lang, 1988. Extremely valuable. Reads like a thesis but covers a lot more than is suggested by its subtitle. Recommended.

Mixner, Manfred. *Peter Handke*. Kronberg: Athenäum, 1977. Essays in German on sundry aspects of Handke's work. Tight text, hard to follow for American readers of German.

Pütz, Peter. *Peter Handke*. Frankfurt: Suhrkamp, 1982. General survey of Handke's books by a modern German literature specialist. Discussions too brief.

Renner, Rolf Günter. *Peter Handke*. Stuttgart: Metzler, 1985. Essays on Handke's work through *Chinese*. For Handke specialists only. Chronological presentation.

Scharang, Michael, ed. *Über Peter Handke*. Frankfurt: Suhrkamp, 1972. Previously published critical accounts, mostly newspaper reviews, of Handke's prose and theater. Dates not always reliable.

Schlueter, June, ed. *The Plays and Novels of Peter Handke*. Pittsburgh: University of Pittsburgh Press, 1981. Excellent survey and discussion of material.

Schultz, Uwe. *Peter Handke*. Velber bie Hannover: Friedrich, 1973. Essays on all the plays.

Articles and Parts of Books

Agena, Kathleen. "Life without Poetry." *Partisan Review* 46, 1 (1979): 126-32. Review of *The Innerworld of the Outerworld of the Innerworld* and *Nonsense and Happiness*. Practical and accessible.

Barry, Thomas F. "In Search of Lost Texts: Memory and the Existential Quest in Peter Handke's *Die Hornissen*." *Seminar* 19, no. 3 (September 1983): 194-214. Excellent article on Handke's first novel. Stresses the existentialist aspect of the book.

Blumer, Arnold. "Peter Handkes romantische Unvernunft." *Acta Germanica* 8 (1973): 123-32. Well-argued but critical of Handke's "newly acquired" role as spokesman for a latter-day romanticism.

Bly, Mark. "Theater in New Haven: Weber on Handke." *Theater* 11, no. 2 (Spring 1980): 83-87. November 1979 interview with the German-born director of Handke's *Unvernünftigen*.

Darby, David. "The Narrative Text as Palimpsest: Levels of discourse in Peter Handke's *Die Hornissen*." *Seminar* 23, no. 3 (September 1987): 251-64. Along with Barry's discussion, one of two standard discussions of Handke's first (difficult) novel.

DeMeritt, Linda C. "Peter Handke: From Alienation to Orientation." *Modern Austrian Literature* 20, no. 1 (1987): 53-71. Handke at a transition point in his work: his move from extreme subjectivity to "orientation."

Demetz, Peter. *After the Fires*. New York: Harcourt Brace Jovanovich, 1986. Contains a chapter on Handke.

Dixon, Christa K. "Peter Handkes *Kaspar*: Ein Modellfall." *German Quarterly* 46, no. 1 (January 1973): 31-46. Early analysis of *Kaspar* as Handke's "model" case of social-linguistic oppression. Standard argument.

Durzak, Manfred. "Zwei charakteristische Neuansätze: Das Romanwerk von Peter Handke und Oswald Wiener." In *Der deutsche Roman der Gegenwart*, 313-39. Stuttgart: Kohlhammer, 1971. Early important survey of Handke's novels by a specialist. Included in a book that discusses Handke as a prose writer among his contemporaries.

Hayman, Ronald. "Peter Handke and the Sentence." In *Theater and Anti-Theater*. New York: Oxford University Press, 1979. Sound, accessible presentation of ideas and theory behind Handke's *Sprechstücke* and two full-length plays.

Hays, Michael. "Peter Handke and the End of the 'Modern.'" *Modern Drama* 23, no. 4 (January 1981): 346-66. Comprehensive, detailed study of Handke's plays. Theory and argument behind the *Sprechstücke* and subsequent plays.

Holzinger, Alfred. "Peter Handkes literarische Anfänge in Graz." In *Wie die Grazer auszogen, die Literatur zu erobern*, edited by Peter Laemmle and Jörg Drews, 183-98. Munich: Lipp, 1975. An account of Handke's early radio and writerly activity in Graz.

Holzinger, Lutz. "Handkes Hörspiele." In *Über Peter Handke*, edited by Michael Scharang. Frankfurt: Suhrkamp. Short survey of Handke's radio plays.

Joseph, Arthur. "Nauseated by Language." *Drama Review* 15, no. 1 (Fall 1990): 57-61.

Kauffmann, Stanley. "Inside Out." *World*, 18 July 1972, 62-65. Discusses Handke's preoccupation in *Die Angst des Tormanns beim Elfmeter* with Wittgenstein's questions about language.

Linstead, Michael. "Peter Handke." In *The Modern German Novel*, edited by Keith Bullivant, 155-70. Leamington Spa: Berg, 1987. Concise summary of the novels through *Chinese*. Recommended as a standard presentation.

Loney, Glenn. "Above the Villages." *Performing Arts Journal* 6, no. 3 (1982): 79-81. Incisive review of the Wenders film of Handke's *Über die Dörfer* (Salzburg Festival).

Marranca, Bonnie. "Peter Handke's *My Foot My Tutor*: Aspects of Modernism." *Michigan Quarterly Review* 16 (1977): 272-79. Focuses on the "silent" aspects of the play.

Mommsen, Katharina. "Peter Handke: *Das Gewicht der Welt* – Tagebuch als literarische Form." In *Peter Handke*, edited by Raimund Fellinger, 242-51. Frankfurt: Suhrkamp, 1985. A discussion of Handke's *Gewicht* as a literary genre.

Nägele, Rainer. "Peter Handke: The Staging of Language." *Modern Drama* 23, no. 4 (January 1981): 327-38. Handke's plays from the aspect of experimental language. Through *Bodensee*.

Peymann, Claus. "Directing Handke." *Drama Review* 16, no. 2 (June 1972): 48-54. A translation of an article in which one of the first European directors of Handke's plays discusses the work from the viewpoint of the director.

Rorrison, Hugh. "The 'Grazer Gruppe,' Peter Handke, and Wolfgang Bauer." In *Modern Austrian Writing*, edited by Alan Best and Hans Wolfschütz, 252-66. London: Wolff, 1980. The background of Handke's early contacts with the founding fathers of Austria's innovative Graz Group and the Forum Stadtpark. Important.

Schlueter, June. " 'Goats and Monkeys' and the 'Idiocy of Language': Handke's *Kaspar* and Shakespeare's *Othello*." *Modern Drama* 23, no. 1 (March 1980): 25-31. Interesting comparative study of language function in Handke's and Shakespeare's plays.

———. "Politics and Poetry: Peter Handke's *They Are Dying Out*." *Modern Drama* 23, no. 4 (January 1981): 339-45. The theme of politics, from an avowedly nonpolitical writer, in *Unvernünftigen*.

Sharp, Francis M. "Peter Handke." In *Major Figures of Contemporary Austrian Literature*, edited by Donald G. Daviau, 207-36. New York: Lang, 1987. Above-average chapter survey of Handke's work through *Chinese*. Contains bibliography.

Weber, Carl. "Handke's Stage Is a Laboratory." *Drama Review* 16, no. 2 (June 1972): 55-62. The director of the American premiere of Handke's *Bodensee* talks about his experience with the actors and the audience of the play.

White, J. J. "Signs of Disturbance: The Semiological Import of Some Recent Fiction by Michel Tournier and Peter Handke." *Journal of European Studies* 4 (1974): 233-54. Handke readers and scholars will value the introduction and discussion of Handke's *Angst* and *Brief* within the context of semiological theory and function. Essential for its clarity and probity.

Bibliographies

Fellinger, Raimund, ed. *Peter Handke*. Frankfurt: Suhrkamp, 1985. The bibliography at the end of the book covers mostly newspaper and journal articles.

Schlueter, June, ed. *The Plays and Novels of Peter Handke*. Pittsburgh: University of Pittsburgh Press, 1981. The bibliography is extensive and standard.

Index

The Author

Richard Arthur Firda attended George Washington University and received his Ph.D. in comparative literature from Harvard University. He then taught at Phillips-Exeter Academy in New Hampshire. At Georgia State University in Atlanta he is a member of the Department of Modern Languages and teaches contemporary German fiction; his secondary research specialties are the modern novel and European feature film. He is the author of *Erich Maria Remarque: An Analysis of His Novels* (1988) and is currently preparing another book on that author.

The Editor

David O'Connell is professor of foreign languages and chair of the Department of Foreign Languages at Georgia State University. He received his Ph.D. from Princeton University in 1966, where he was a National Woodrow Wilson Fellow, the Bergen Fellow in Romance Languages, and a National Woodrow Wilson Dissertation Fellow. He is the author of *The Teachings of Saint Louis: A Critical Text* (1972), *Les Propos de Saint Louis* (1974), *Louis-Ferdinand Céline* (1976), *The Instructions of Saint Louis: A Critical Text* (1979), and *Michel de Saint Pierre: A Catholic Novelist at the Crossroads* (1990). He is the editor of *Catholic Writers in France since 1945* (1983) and has served as review editor (1977-79) and managing editor (1987-90) of the *French Review*.